D1716041

Original Cover Design by Steve Bass
Final Cover Design by Mascot Books
Book Design and Layout by Jankowski Design

Photography and food styling:
Nita Desai, under direction of Jerry Jankowski

www.mascotbooks.com

Simply Indian: Vegetarian Cuisine of Western India

All material in *Simply Indian: Vegetarian Cuisine of Western India* is provided as information only and should not be construed as medical advice or instruction. Readers should consult appropriate health professionals on any matter relating to their health, nutrition, and well-being. It is the reader's responsibility to determine the value and quality of any recipe or instructions provided for food preparation and to determine the nutritional value, if any, and safety of the preparation instructions. The author and publisher make no representation or warranties with respect to the accuracy or completeness of the contents of the cookbook.

For more information, please contact:
Mascot Books
620 Herndon Parkway, Suite 320
Herndon, VA 20170
info@mascotbooks.com

CPSIA Code: PRTWP1017A
ISBN-13: 978-1-68401-313-5

Printed in Korea

TRADITIONAL FAMILY RECIPES SIMPLIFIED FOR TODAY'S BUSY WORLD

SIMPLY INDIAN

 Vegetarian Cuisine of Western India 

NITA DESAI

This book is dedicated to my mother, Santokben Prabhudas Mehta, who taught me how to cook with passion, love, positive thoughts, and joy.

We are gifted with five senses – sight, sound, smell, touch, and taste. There is nothing more powerful to arouse these senses than food and flavorful cooking.

"I have the simplest tastes. I am always satisfied with the best."
Oscar Wilde

"Food is our common ground, a universal experience."
James Beard

"Food is a central activity of mankind and one of the single most significant trademarks of a culture."
Mark Kurlansky

"You have to know the culture to taste the food."
Author unknown

"Food is culture, habit, creativity, and identity."
Author unknown

"Cooking food is a central activity of the kitchen and one of the most significant passions of mankind."
Author unknown

"There is no love sincerer than the love of food."
George Bernard Shaw, *Man and Superman*

"You are what what you eat eats."
Michael Pollan

"One cannot think well, love well, sleep well, if one has not dined well."
Author unknown

"You don't need a silver fork to eat good food."
Paul Prudhomme

Table of Contents

Welcome to Simply Indian

Four burners are going at the same time on the stove in my kitchen. Rice is cooking on one, vegetables on another. Spices are sizzling in oil on the fourth, sending out rich aromas of black mustard seeds, cumin methi, cloves, and curry leaves.

The dough for the puris is on the side ready for cooking, as is the batter for the pakoras.

We are having company for dinner. The menu will include kadhi, sprouted mug, boondi raita, mixed vegetables kachumber, kheer, cauliflower pakoras and vegetables masaledar with cilantro, grated coconut garlic, and spices. All this will be accompanied by puris and two freshly made condiments.

Right now you may not know how those dishes taste, but by the time you finish this cook book, you will know, and your mouth will salivate in anticipation.

Welcome to my kitchen: the place where I have enjoyed some of my happiest moments. I am in my element here, orchestrating a meal for many, the bowls filled with prepared ingredients.

Cooking is my pleasure and has been since I was a child. I grew up in a large extended Indian family – at least twenty people sat down to dinner together every day in our home – in a small town with very few modern amenities. My five sisters and I picked stones and sticks and pebbles from grains before they were oiled and stored, competing with each other as to who had cleaned the most. We helped my mother and aunt roast corn on an open stove, adding lemon juice and chile powder. We helped peel, cut, and shred mangoes – hundreds of them – to pickle, sun dry, salt and / or sweeten with a special blend of spices to make many varieties of preserves and condiments which were stored in apothecary jars and lasted for the whole year. We helped grind spices into powders and roll and flatten the dough just the right way for the family's breads.

The cooking facilities were a far cry from what is available today. Indian cooking was done on brick or iron stoves fueled by coal. There were no ovens, no electric stoves, and no refrigerators available outside the big cities.

The one thing that was the same as today was the joy we had in cooking. My parents believed cooking should be fun. No matter how rich or poor you are, they told us, wherever you go you will have to feed your family, so it's best to enjoy cooking, rather than make it a chore.

My mother even took the theme one step further: "If you're happy when you cook," she said, "the good thoughts and happiness will go into the food you make."

If this is true, I have been passing on happiness and good thoughts all my life.

When I arrived in the United States, my husband and his brothers lived in a small apartment with a kitchen that contained only one pot and two skillets. The day I came, they begged me to cook a real Indian meal, which was quite a challenge. I finally managed to find the fresh spices and proper flour I needed some thirty miles away in an Armenian store on Sunset Boulevard.

Having so many different cultures in India, it is a wonderful experience to see and taste the variety of foods for each festival. The style, the colors and the aroma may vary from region to region, but the sense of specialty and hospitality exists in all regions.

When we moved to northern California we were surrounded by many young couples like us who had recently migrated from India. All of a sudden we had a large group of close friends and many, many cooperative efforts to create potluck Indian dinners where the taste competition was fierce, recipes were shared, and my recipe collection grew.

By then I had two children and many more family members who had arrived to study. It is an Indian tradition that if any guest or friend is in the house at meal time, his or her place is set and that person cannot leave without having something to eat. There were weekends when we found ourselves entertaining about fifteen guests, all of whom were dying for a "homecooked" Indian meal.

We moved to Malaysia where I broadened my expertise, learning how to cook Malaysian, Thai, South Indian, and Chinese recipes. I also worked on my first cookbook, one put together by the American Association there, and, at the request of the Indian Association, began holding cooking classes.

When we returned to the United States, I became a realtor, and therefore a "working mother" who loved to cook, but had to fit her passion into a very full schedule. That did not stop the experimentation – the constant search for a better recipe or a faster, easier way to make a traditional one. I have always invited our friends and our children's friends over to serve as my tasters, and it is these tasters who have encouraged me to put together this cookbook.

Indian cooking has come a long way since my youth. One of the items we made fresh every day was green chutney, since it was a vital addition to any meal and we had no refrigeration to preserve it from day to day. To make it we had to grind fresh green chilies, fresh ginger, and lots of cilantro with both hands using a rounded stone. The yield was only one bowl and the labor was intensive. Today, of course, with the convenience of food processors, you can mix everything in the blender to exactly the right consistency in a few minutes, store it for days in the refrigerator, or freeze it for months. The chutney still tastes delicious, and makes both a great food accompaniment – and an exotic sandwich spread as well.

I differ from my forebears in the ease with which I am able to cook - thanks to modern appliances and modern food stores - and also in the way some of my food is prepared. The vegetables I grew up eating were well spiced but dull in color and overly soft in texture – probably because they had to be overcooked for health reasons. The recipes you will find in this book will not only turn out to be tasty; they will be beautiful as well. Vision enhances taste. So does scent. As a result, I pay special attention to color and aroma.

You will also be able to make them in much less time. *Simply Indian* is a book of shortcuts, a cookbook for anyone who has a career, family, busy and full life, and still wants to know how to prepare delicious meals.

Nita Desai, Chef and Author

About Indian Food | The Regions

REGIONS OF INDIA

1. Northern India
Wheat, onions, tomatoes, and other vegetables are used daily. For non-vegetarians, the main items are lamb / mutton and chicken. The bread made in Tandoor is a specialty of Northern India, influenced by Muslim culture since Moguls ruled the area for many years. Tandoor Naan is very popular among Indians and Westerners alike.

2. Eastern India
Fish, rice, and coconut, along with milk and yogurt, are main ingredients of food in this area, which extends from the middle portion of India past Bangladesh. The region of Bangal is known for special sweets made from milk. Rasgula (Roshagula) is the most popular, made with white milk balls in syrup.

3. Central India
(Madhya Pradesh)
Food in this area is influenced by all four surrounding regions. Main ingredients and dishes are similar to Gujarat. Due to previous Mogul influence, this region boasts of biryani, korma, kheema, and kababs, which are very special for non-vegetarians. Special sweet dish Jalebi is very popular.

4. Western India
This area has moderate rain to desert areas. Staple food is bread made from millet or wheat, vegetables, legumes and homemade yogurt. Village-style food is very popular and there are special restaurants that serve this type of fare.

5. Southern India
The staple food is fish and rice in the region along the coast. Due to the gentle hills and rain, there are hundreds of rice fields. Coconut grows in abundance and thus has become the main ingredient in preparing food. Rice, vegetables, and curry made with coconut milk would be for vegetarians. You can smell the aroma of coconut oil in most restaurants. Roti is sometimes served with South Indian meals.

To understand Indian food, it is important to know about the different regions of India. Each region boasts its own food, culture, and traditions. There are non-vegetarians and vegetarians in each region.

Most vegetarians do not eat chicken, fish, or eggs. Each region has its staple food, chosen because of weather, terrain, and culture.

The food is generally spicy and hot in most areas, and yogurt is used almost daily.

The spices and vegetarian diet were created thousands of years ago using Ayurvedic science. Many Indian spices have great medicinal qualities.

Lunch is usually the main meal in India, and the evening meal is generally light.

The Differences Between Regional Foods

You may wonder, how can I tell what Indian dishes come from where?

- Most southern Indian food will have coconut milk as its sauce base.
- Most northern Indian food will have cream or yogurt as its sauce base.
- In the western part of India, where I come from, yogurt is used on a daily basis.
- Most people along the coast add fish to their otherwise vegetarian meals.
- The people who live in the northern region also stray from a vegetarian diet by adding chicken and mutton or lamb to their dishes.
- An Indian vegetarian diet does not contain fish, chicken, or eggs.

About Indian Food | The Basics

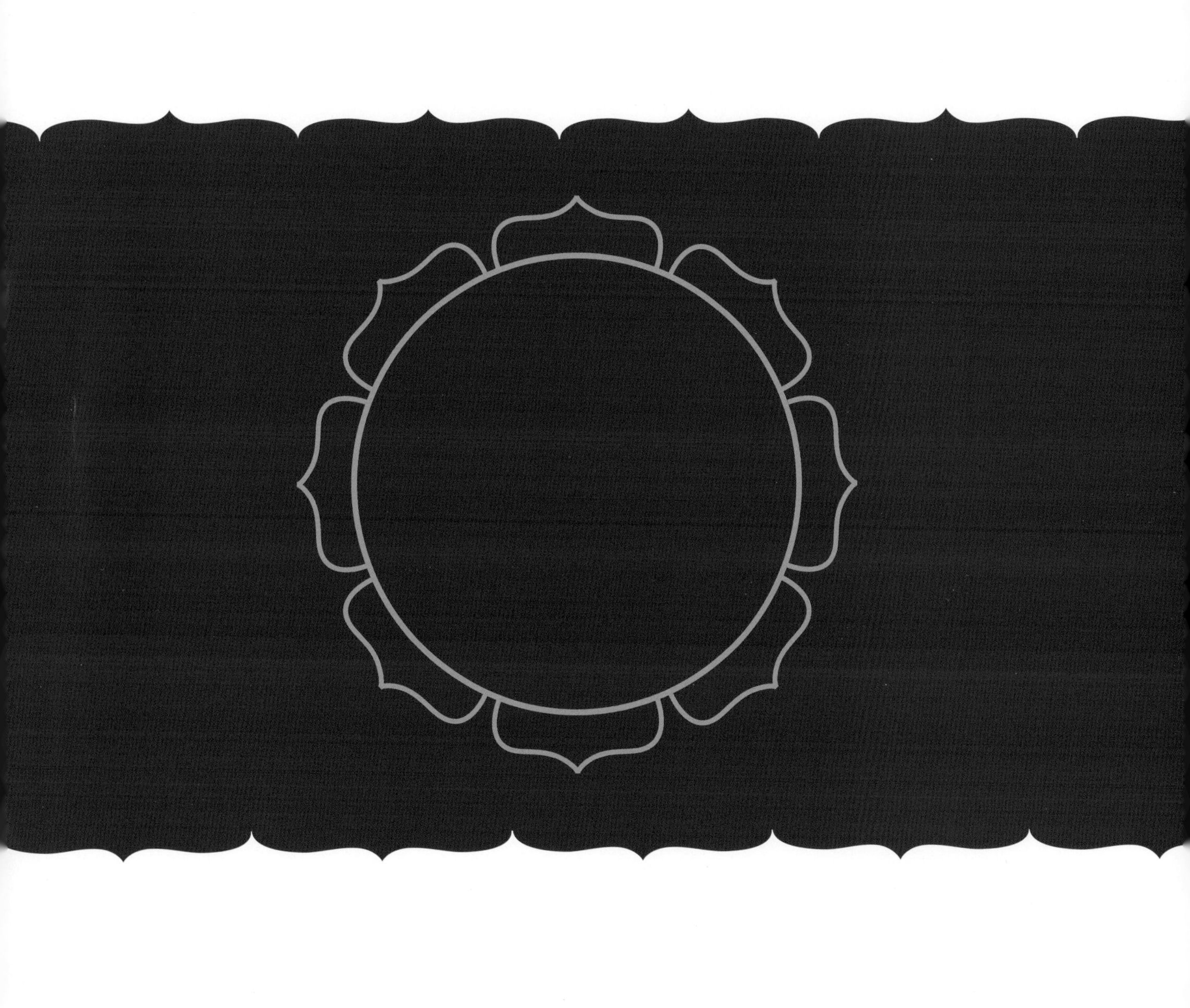

About Indian Food | The Basics

India is known for its hospitality and culturally diverse food. In different communities throughout the country, the customs for preparing, serving, and eating vary. When you are invited into an Indian home, you will be the first one served at the table. Being served second and third helpings of food is normal. If you are accustomed to eating what you want and as much or as little as you want of it, this may take some getting used to.

The Indian style for eating is not consuming one food item at a time, as in Western customs. Indian meals are a blend of many items and flavors. A piece of roti is often used to scoop up vegetables and other items in small portions for one very flavorful bite.

Indian food is not complex to make, once you know how to use some of the basic spices. The chapter on spices explains which spices are used most often. The simplicity and organization of the spice box is a perfect tool for any aspiring Indian cook.

It is also important for you to learn about unfamiliar ingredients before you start cooking with them. If you are new to cooking Indian food, it would be a good idea to begin with simple dishes.

Scooping daal.

Cooking is an art, so use your creativity and artistic talents to create whatever food you like and to serve it in an appealing way.

Many recipes in this book are vegan also and many are gluten-free. In some recipes, coconut can be used in stead of yogurt—alternate recipes are given with the recipe.

Daals, Vegetable, Kachumber and some other recipes which have sugar can be substituted with agave nectar.

Sugar cuts tanginess and, in some cases, spicy hot taste.

Chai

Chai – sweet, milky tea with complementing spices—is by far the most popular drink in India. It can be consumed at any time, but especially in the morning and afternoon. This spicy drink is served hot. The unique blend of loose black tea and spices, which varies in different regions of the country, is first boiled in water with milk.

In recent years, many coffee and tea specialty manufacturers have been marketing this drink in the U.S. and other countries. Tea that is used to make chai should be from India for an authentic flavor and taste. Mamri–loose black tea—is a flavorful and popular variety that can be purchased in any Indian market

Chai is made with milk, but for the lactose intolerant, soy or almond milk can be used. Add these substitutes when serving. Do not boil soy or almond milk.

Nita's Special Chai

Since the late 1990s, Chai has become a very popular drink in Western countries. In India, the word "chai" simply means "ready tea." Generally, chai is made using loose black tea, water, milk, sugar, and a blend of fresh or dried spices boiled together. Each family may have their own choice of spice blend. This simple recipe is always a crowd pleaser in my home and a favorite of my guests.

Some recipes vary the amounts of the spices shown below, but most masala chai will have these five ingredients and sometimes nutmeg. Nutmeg and star anise are the signature spices of some well-known coffee shops. I chose to leave out the nutmeg because it has a reputation for making people drowsy. In the winter months, my chai is a great way to warm up.

Chai Spice Blend (all ingredients are ground or in powder form):

4 oz. dried ginger
2 oz. black pepper
2 oz. cardamom
1 oz. cinnamon
1 oz. clove

CHAI WITH KHAKRA

How to make chai:

- Bring 3 cups of water to a boil. Add 3 teaspoons of loose black tea and ⅛ to ¼ teaspoon of the Chai Spice Blend. Add 1 cup milk and bring to a second boil. Cover and let the spices and tea steep for about 5 minutes. This opens the leaves of the tea and releases the flavor.
- Remove from the heat source. Strain and serve with sugar or honey to taste. You can keep it warm in a thermos. Soy, almond, or coconut milk can be used instead of milk for those who are lactose intolerant. Add this before serving. Do not boil soy, coconut, or almond milk.

Chick Pea Flour (Chana Flour) Basen

Chana flour or *basen*, made from chickpeas (also known as garbanzo beans), is used as a thickening agent for sauces and a batter for *pakoras* (fritters). This flour should be stored in a cool, dry place. Savory snacks like *boondi* are also made from *chana* flour, and it does not contain gluten.

Chana flour is available in either fine or coarse varieties. The fine variety is used to make sauces and batters.

Chutney

For the average American, *chutney* is something of a mystery food. This is partially due to the fact that it can be sweet, very spicy, or both. It can have the consistency of Mexican salsa or be dense like hummus. The main ingredient is usually what the chutney will be called: coconut chutney, tamarind chutney, garlic chutney, date chutney, etc. The spices that are commonly used in chutneys are cumin, coriander / cilantro, mint, and tamarind. Cilantro/coriander and mint are hari chutneys. The British created their own version of chutney using mango, raisins, vinegar, onion, lime juice, and tamarind as the major ingredients.

Citric Acid

Sometimes when you're cooking *daals*, vegetables, curries, or some snacks that require a tangy taste, but lemon juice is not available, citric acid can be used.

Coconut

Special tools are needed to break open the hard shell to get at the coconut inside. After the coconut meat is removed, it can then be shredded. Most of the cooking in southern India requires freshly grated coconut and coconut milk. In the U.S., local stores generally carry sweetened coconut. This is not the preferred version for Indian cooking. You may also find shredded coconut in the frozen section of Asian or Indian markets.

If the shredded coconut is in a large frozen lump, you may have to partially thaw it. Fill a deep pan with enough water to just cover however much coconut you are using. Heat until warm, but do not boil. Let the coconut sit in the water for 2 to 5 minutes. Pour the contents through the strainer. Press down on the coconut to remove the water, then transfer the strained coconut to a bowl and use as directed.

Canned coconut milk is available in US grocery stores or Asian markets.

Coconut Milk

Coconut is the most common garnish for vegetables, rice, and many other dishes in Indian cuisine. You can eat it with chopped, fresh cilantro. Most regions along the coast in India use coconut more prominently in their dishes, since this fruit is available in abundance. Coconut milk can be used as a curry base and can be diluted with witer. It is used in many Indian dishes. Coconut also has health and healing properties. Drinking coconut water has health and healing effects.

In India, nothing is wasted – coconut water and the whole coconut have uses. Coconut milk is actually the milky juice of a ripe coconut that is squeezed after grating. Young coconuts are sold in many stores throughout India, and people use the coconut water to cool themselves in hot weather, when tender young coconut pulp is a special treat. After using the inside of the coconut, furthermore, the hard shell can be made into decorative items or bowls. The outside husk is typically used for heating fuel in the villages and rural areas of India.

Top: Coconut broken apart showing meat inside.

Bottom: Using a seive or stainer to squeeze out moisture from grated coconut.

Condiments are set out as accompaniments to main meals and are generally served with small spoons. Some condiments are hot and spicy, some sweet and spicy, and some freshly made—not hot or spicy.

Most homes have a condiment tray with several bowls of different varieties. Some homes have as many as 10 or 12 types of condiments. Pictured here is a tray containing eight condiments.

Coconut Oil

Coconut oil has been used for frying in southern India for centuries. Coconut oil, which gives fried food a different flavor than any other cooking or frying oil, is available in most Indian and, many US grocery stores. Use only virgin non-hydrogenated coconut oil for cooking or frying. We will also be using freshly grated and squeezed coconut in many recipes in this book.

Condiments

Most Indian families will offer a tray with five to nine or even more small bowls that are filled with different condiments with every meal. This tray is different from family to family and between communities. Some condiments are preserved, and some are fresh. Most preserved condiments are pickles.

The typical fresh condiments are mainly *chutneys*, freshly made pickles or achars, fresh ginger, fresh turmeric, fresh peppers, and cut lemon or lime (to be squeezed on food). Salt and other special items can be added separately. The condiments should be regarded as a taste enhancer for the meals that are being served — some sour, some sweet, some hot, some sweet and hot, and so on. Generally, condiments are served with main meals and not as snack dishes or sweets. Typically a spoonful or two of any condiment is sufficient for a person.

Coriander Leaves Cilantro (Kothmari, or Hara Dhania)

This fresh herb is used daily in preparing and serving Indian foods such as vegetables, *daals*, pilafs, and savory items. It is sometimes used while cooking and often as a garnish.

It is extremely important to wash cilantro before using it. Fill a bowl with cold water and cut the stems off about two inches from the bottom while the bunch is still tied. Untie the bunch and immerse it in the water. Gently stir. With both hands, gently remove the loose stems with leaves and put them into a colander. Let the water drain, then take the bunch and chop it fine. It is important that the chopped coriander is dry before it is stored in a container. There are containers available at markets in which to store fresh coriander.

Coriander leaves.

Cream of Wheat (Sooji)

Cream of wheat is also known as "sooji" or "rava." It comes in three different grades of coarseness – fine, medium, and large. The fine variety is used for breads: it is added to dough or batter that is too watery. It will make the dough or batter thicker.

Experienced cooks find cream of wheat invaluable. The medium variety is used to make *halva* or *shira*, *uttapam*, and *rava dosa*. The coarse variety is also used for *halva*, depending on personal preferences, as well as for *upma*, *rava idli*, and other dishes. In the U.S., these three varieties are available in many markets. It is best to refrigerate them so that they keep for a long time.

Curry

Curry is another food item that Westerners are often confused about. As contradictory as it may seem, curry powder is not generally made from curry leaves. Curry powder is a blend of dry spices. Curry itself, on the other hand, is a thick sauce made with ingredients such as onions, tomatoes, garlic, and other ingredients that are sautéed and then blended to make a paste.

Different regions in India have different types of curry. A very popular one is curry from the northern part of India that uses above ingredients with cream. The vibrant color indicates freshness of the curry. Southern Indian cuisine uses coconut milk along with green chilies, ginger, cumin, curry leaves, and other spices.

Varieties of daals. Top to bottom: Urad, mung, masoor, urad, chana, and tuvar.

Above: Daal simmering on the stovetop.

Daals (Beans and Legumes)

Many people think of beans in terms of the Mexican pinto or the navy bean varieties. However, there are many varieties of beans (and legumes) that are grown and used in India. *Daals* (or *dhals*) are beans that have been split. The word daal also refers to the thick stew made from split or whole beans and can be combined with various other types of beans, lentils, or peas. Most daals are made with only one kind of daal bean each, but there are also mixed daals of three or more types depending on the cook's creativity in the region of specialty.

Sprouted whole beans have a unique and wholesome nutty taste. For vegetarians in India—more than half the population—the best source for protein is daal. Most sprouted beans make great toppings to add to salads — raw or cooked.

The many varieties of daals are made differently, depending on the region. Different families may have their own favorite or special recipes. *Mung daal* is made from split mung beans, and it is the easiest to prepare for new or novice cooks. *Tuvar daal* is one of the most common *daals* made daily in many homes; is made from split yellow lentils. *Chana daal* is made from split chickpeas. Most daals are soaked from half an hour to overnight before cooking, depending on the type.

Whole beans will need 8 to 10 hours of soaking, while split beans will need half an hour to a few hours of soaking. Because daal contains a lot of protein, it requires being cooked thoroughly. The use of oil, such as *tadka*, is also important in making daal.

Garnishes (clockwise from top): Chopped cilantro, coconut, tomatoes, onions, sunflower seeds, and red bell pepper.

Dates

Dates are a dried fruit that is typically associated with the Middle East. They are used in making chutneys and as a sweetener when cooking. Pitted dates are first soaked for about half an hour and then boiled for about 5 to 10 minutes to soften. A paste is made from the boiled dates, with use of a blender, and spices can be added to make chutney. Dates are considered by Ayurvedic gurus to be a good source of vitamin E. This is a great substitute for sugar in daals and curries.

Dates are also used to add to many sweets like *payasam* or *kheer*. Many sweets are made using dates and mixed nuts.

Note: Buy pitted dates to save time and soak them overnight in water. Boil to soften them, and make a smooth paste in the blender, adding spices.

Garnish tray

A colorful garnish really makes food look appetizing. Most cooked foods, especially vegetables, daals, curries, and some side dishes, may look alike in color, so using right garnish is important. A garnish tray generally consists of chopped fresh coriander or cilantro, shredded chopped tomatoes, chopped onions, and chopped green chilies. These are mainly used to garnish vegetables, daals, curries, and savory side dishes.

Chopped or ground nuts, dried fruits, and ground cardamom seeds are generally used to garnish sweet dishes. Saffron is added just before the food is dished out in the serving bowl, as this gives it its most vibrant color. For best results, add saffron on top of mix in the sweet dish and cover for about 5 minutes before serving. Adding it while cooking may cause its color to fade.

Use of Fruit Salt

Fruit salt is often used instead of baking soda. It seems to work well in pakoras and other items that may require baking soda. Fruit salt in powder form, which gives good results, is available in jars in Indian Markets.

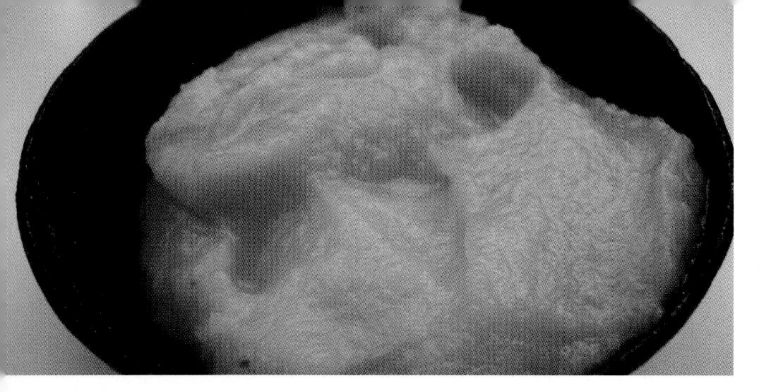

Ghee (Recipe included in "Everything Else" chapter)

There are several varieties of rice available in India, not just basmati.

Freshly roasted papodams.

Ghee (Clarified Butter)

Clarified butter is also used in many Western and French dishes. It is used every day on roti instead of butter and as the fat for *tadka* and daals. Ghee is an item of controversy for "healthy" cooking, though. Ayurvedic medicine recommends the use of ghee because the fatty acids are supposed to be healthy, but modern medicine claims that ghee is high in cholesterol and saturated fats. Many recipes in this book that use ghee also mention if oil can be used as a substitute.

Ghee heats quickly, and you should be vigilant when using ghee for tadka.

Ginger-Chili Paste

This is a common paste used in most daal and vegetable recipes as well as with snack foods like *samosas* and *pakoras*. Ginger-chili paste is easy to make and can be stored in the refrigerator for days. Add the amount of chili according to your taste. There is no standard measure; different families have different preferences for hot food. Generally, a four-inch piece of chopped ginger and 2 to 3 whole seeded jalapeños would be a good start. Adjust the hotness as desired.

What is Khakra?

This crispy roti was created to use up the leftover roti that was made the night before.

To make khakra, leftover roti are put on a heated roti pan at low heat, one at a time. This process is time-consuming and the roti have to be pressed with a cloth so they stay flat.

Khakra is easy to find in Indian markets. There are several varieties available.

Many community and religious organizations in India give jobs to women to make this special, time-consuming item, since they have the patience and the skill for it. Khakra are extremely thin and crispy. Although they make a great snack anytime, people usually serve them in the morning with tea.

An assortment of very sweet, colorful desserts, some made with dairy products and some made without.

Oils for cooking

Any oil that is your favorite is a good oil to use, but it is also important to know the properties of oils when frying and cooking. All oils are not the same when heated to high temperatures. Hydrogenated oil is not used in this book.

I personally like to cook with grape seed oil and use olive oil for salads. Peanut oil, sesame seed oil, mustard oil, and ginger oil are used in different regions of India. Coconut oil is very popular in southern India and is used in daily cooking and frying. Get to know the qualities of an oil before using it to cook for guests. Daals, breads (roti), and vegetables are all cooked with some oil. Many condiments are also prepared with oil, because it works as a preservative. Oil is used to preserve Indian pickles, or (*achars*). Oil also enhances the taste in savory items and give texture to vegetable dishes.

Papadums

Papadums are among the most popular snacks for adults and children. Some are spicy, some are not. Making papadums is difficult and time-consuming. In many community organizations, they are made by the ladies to help give women jobs. Indian markets carry a variety of them.

Papadums are made from *urad* or moong daal or rice. Flour is made from one of these daals. The dough is made using water, spices, salt, and a cooking soda. It is then pounded, softened, and made into balls that are flattened and rolled thin, and sun dried before packing. Packets of *papadums* are available in Indian and other ethnic food stores. *Papadums* can be roasted on a traditional open flame or deep-fried. They can also be roasted in the toaster oven or microwave. If you have never roasted papadums before, use the microwave or deep-fry them. Roasting them on an open flame requires careful handling.

Rice

Rice is a staple in the diets of many Indian households. In the western world, the most popular kind of Indian rice is basmati rice, available in most supermarkets. "Basmati" means "fragrant" in Hindi. Basmati rice grains are longer than average rice grains. The grains of basmati rice are not sticky when cooked with the right amount of time with the right amount of water.

Basmati rice has been aged for three years or more and will last for a long time in your pantry. Basmati rice is considered a rich man's rice. Several varieties of rice are available in Indian markets. Certain kinds of rice are preferred for particular recipes, and using basmati rice may not bring the same good results.

Indian rice varieties in Indian markets include Shri Lanka rice, Kerala red rice or Sona Msoori, Surti kolam, and other types. These and brown rice are unpolished rice, and require more water and time to cook.

Rice is generally scrubbed clean in a bowl of water by hand, soaked, and drained before cooking. Soaking time depends up the kind of rice used.

Information for soaking and cooking time for Rice is covered in "Rice" Chapter.

Storing Dry Goods

Most dry foods, like daals and rice, may last a long time if they are stored in dry, airtight jars. Be careful to check the jars if you have not used them in a long time to make sure that bugs have not taken over. It is good to wash daals and rice before cooking. Most flour can last a long time if it is stored in a dry and cool place, but some whole wheat flour may become stale, especially if it has already been stored on the shelf for a long time. Wheat flour stored in the refrigerator stays fresh longer.

Sweets

If you are lactose intolerant or allergic to any dairy product, be cautious, as most Indian sweets are made using milk or butter. Sweets are made with nuts, coconut, *chana* flour or wheat flour, and some form of dairy product.

Note: Most Indian sweets tend to be extra sweet. Try a small piece or portion at first, before you find that you've taken more than you care to eat.

Tadka

Tadka is a process of enhancing the flavor in daals and vegetables. In *daals*, this process is performed after the daals are cooked.

In vegetables, it is done before cooking. A little oil is heated in a pan and sprinkled with black mustard seeds, cumin seeds, red dry chili, cloves, cinnamon, and /or curry leaves. How these ingredients are used depends not only on the cook but on the items themselves; when it comes to flavor. Some of these ingredients blend best with certain others to release better flavors. Most commonly used spices for *tadka* are cumin, black mustard seeds, and curry leaves.

Tapioca

Also known as "sabudana," this dish comes in different sizes: small, medium, and large. We have used the medium size in this book. Sabudana are starch balls that can be used to make a sweet dish like kheer, added to potatoes to make *tikki*, and used with potatoes to make *sabudan khichdi*. You can also find sabudana wafers like papadums in Indian stores, and you can make these at home by frying your tapioca. Remember that sabudana must be soaked for half an hour before use.

Whole Wheat Flour

Several varieties of this flour are available in Indian stores. The whole wheat flour available in U.S. supermarkets tends to be difficult to use for Indian flat bread as they are of a coarse variety. The fine variety of wheat flour is good for making roti and available in Indian markets. Most households use this flour without leavening in preparing the dough for flat breads.

Along the West Coast, the staple bread is made of corn and wheat flour, although some Western areas use millet to make bread. Bread made from millet is heavier and denser than bread made from wheat flour because it has to be thicker to prevent it from falling apart. If you are new at making roti, it is easier to start with regular wheat flour.

Yogurt

Most Indian households make their own yogurt at home, but if you like, you can buy plain unsweetened yogurt in grocery stores almost anywhere in the U.S. The simple method of making yogurt is listed in "Everything Else" chapter, and you don't need an electric yogurt-maker. Yogurt is used in many different ways in the Indian diet. Traditionally, it is used with meals, sweets, raita, vegetables, and daals. Sweet and salted drinks are also made with yogurt. Yogurt has been known for its probiotic health qualities for thousands of years.

Utensils and gadgets

Almost every kitchen in India includes a pressure cooker, a tadka pot, a rolling pin (thinner than the one typically used in Western countries), a rolling board (round-shaped), a deep-frying pot (like a wok), a spice box, a strainer, a colander, a spatula, and an Indian whisk. If you expect to make roti often, you should purchase a roti skillet. Roti skillets are round, have no raised edge, and are somewhat rounded at the bottom. The cast iron and nonstick varieties are usually available in Indian stores. I prefer cast iron because of its greater longevity and the superior cooking experience it offers. If you are a frequent ghee user, you can find a ghee bowl in specialty stores.

INDIAN ROLLING PIN
INDIAN WISK
DEEP FRYER SPATULA
SPATULA
TONGS
SANSI POT HOLDER

Colorful and popular falooda dessert topped with nuts and takmaria.

Use of Nuts and Dried Fruits

Indian sweets are known to have some nuts and dried fruit in them. Please check for allergies to any of the nuts before eating or serving these.

Most Indian sweet dishes are garnished with crushed (raw or blanched) almonds and pistachios, raisins, walnuts, and cashews. The raisins used are not the dark brown ones that are common in Western countries, but the lighter variety: golden raisins.

- Cashews are also used to make some northern Indian dishes. Chopped dry figs and dates are also used for garnishing. Peanuts are used whole or, in some dishes like *tadka*, roasted and ground; otherwise roasted ones are used most of the time.
- Use of peanuts: When used ground the recipe, use roasted, when using whole- generally used in *tadka*, raw peanuts are OK.
- Any nuts used for garnishing are generally chopped or crushed.

Black raisins, not black currants, are sometimes soaked in water and eaten as a cooling food in very moderate amounts. I remember eating them during the summer. These raisins are also used in cooking and healthy drinks.

Dried figs are used for garnishes and to make some sweets.

Dates are used mainly for chutneys and sweets, and for adding sweetness to curries and daals.

Almonds and pistachios are used often. These nuts are chopped, sliced, or ground to sprinkle as garnishes or added to sweet dishes while cooking. Cashews, almonds, and pistachios are ground to make special sweets during festivals.

Cooking Tips and Useful Gadgets

Pressure Cooker

The pressure cooker is very useful tool in Indian cooking. Most families' daily midday meal consists of daal and rice with vegetables and roti. Using a pressure cooker to make these items is very easy, as the cooker has timed whistles and keeps the food warm until it is opened. Most families will cook their daal, rice, potatoes, and / or other vegetables in a pressure cooker. It is a time saver, and it also comes with compartments so that items can be steam-cooked separately.

Pressure cookers are available in most department or kitchen stores. The key is to how to use the device. Most Indian families learn how to use the device. Most Indian families generally have a pressure cooker, no matter where they are in the world. This is a cultural aspect of Indian cooking.

Indian Utensils

Most countries have their special cooking utensils, and India is the same. The rolling pad and rolling pin are probably the best examples of this. The pots, pot holders, spatulas, flat roti pan, Indian whisk, tongs, serving spoon, and many others implements are other examples. Pictures of these are shown to let you know what they look like and their typical uses. Some utensils can be substituted, if you are accustomed to different ones. Most of these are available in Indian stores.

Use of Modern Electric Gadgets

You may already have some of these gadgets which are used for similar process; it is okay to use them as long as they serve the requirements for you.

- A hand mixer with a long handle can be used for making *tuvar daal*; a yogurt whisk for *kadhi* and other sauces.
- A dry-grinding coffee grinder works well if you are going to grind your own spices. It's a good idea to clean it after using, or your coffee may taste a bit wrong.
- Regular blender. You may be able to use this more often if you get one with a small chopping cup. A small chopper can work as well, but a blender is a very useful gadget for making chutneys and other items.
- A chopper — electric, if possible — is great for making chutneys, ginger-chili paste, and other quick items.
- A few prep bowls in small to medium sizes will be very helpful in preparing many dishes.
- Spoons. I've found that cooking is easier if you have lots of small spoons ready. You can put them in a mug and use them as needed.

Time-Saving Items

For time-saving and convenience, many store-bought items are used in this book. I buy these items and keep them ready at all times. They are available in many Indian or specialty stores and supermarkets.

- Ginger garlic paste – You can buy it in a market or make your own and freeze it in small containers. I generally make ginger garlic paste and ginger-chili paste and freeze them in ice cube trays. These cubes can then be stored in small freezer bags.
- Ginger-chili paste
- Grated coconut — The frozen variety is best.
- Dalia (roasted, split chickpeas) – used for chutneys, tadka, and other processes.
- Tomato chutney or curry sauce
- Peanuts, almonds, cashews, pistachios, saffron, golden raisins, dried cranberries, sunflower seeds, and pumpkin seeds (*pepita*) — These can be stored in plastic bags or small containers and used as often as you desire. Be creative, adding these items for taste, crunch, and color. Please check for relevant allergies before serving.
- Spice box — THE MOST IMPORTANT ITEM to keep on hand. This box contains the spices, both ground and whole, that an Indian cook uses on a daily basis. This box has been a part of my cooking routine ever since I started cooking in my own kitchen.

Pressure cooker with beans.

Indian Spices

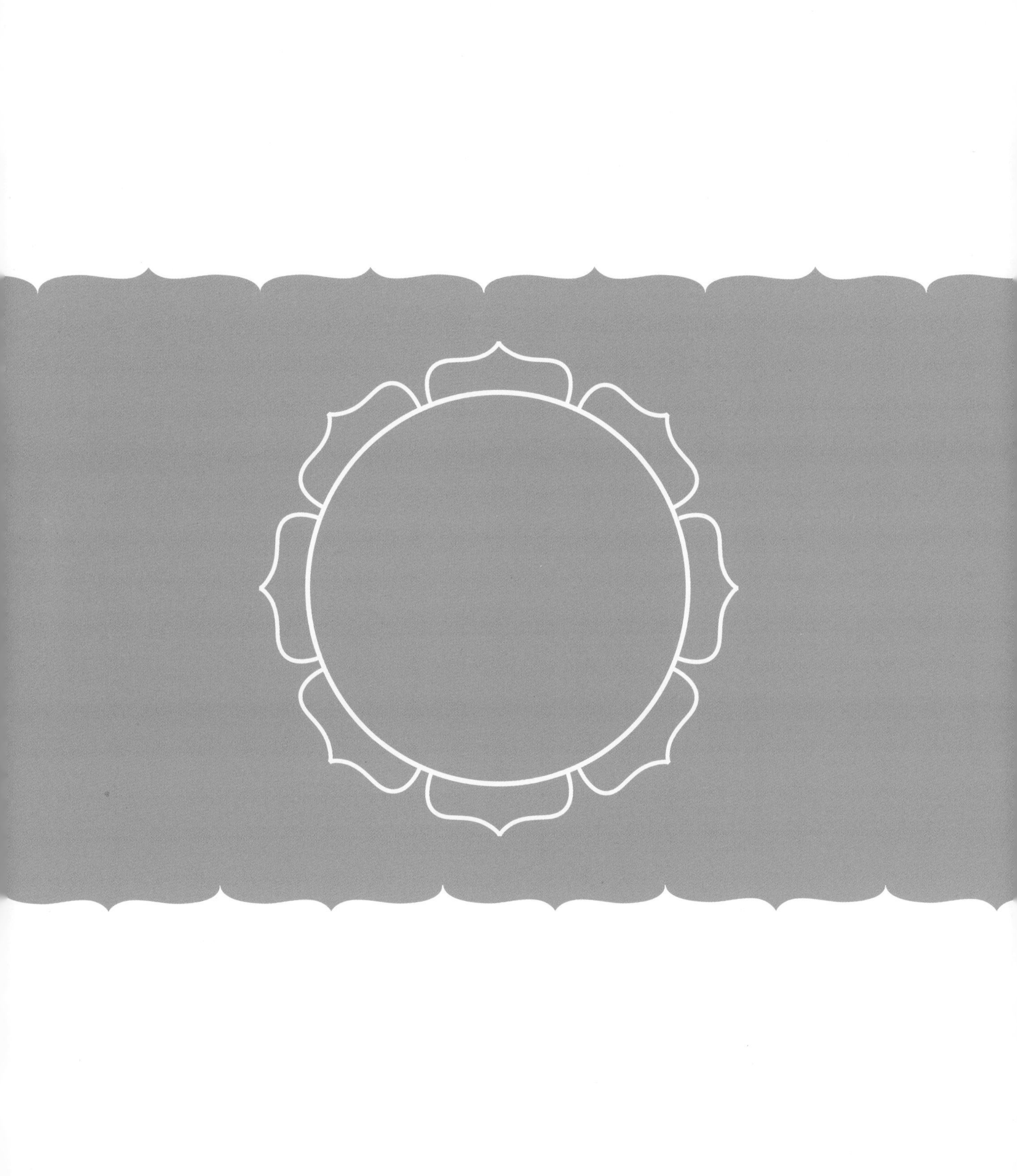

Indian Spices

Spice box (clockwise from top to bottom): Tumeric, black mustard, cumin seeds, kokum, chili, dhana jeera. Middle spice: Dry whole chilies, cinnamon sticks, cloves, and curry leaves.

The spices that are used in preparing Indian food come directly from plants that originated in Asia and Africa, from their roots (turmeric and ginger), bark (cinnamon and lemon grass), leaves (curry leaves, basil leaves, bay leaves, *kasoori methi*—dried fenugreek leaves—and cilantro), flowers (saffron), and fruits (chilies, paprika, nutmeg, anise, black cumin, black pepper, cloves). These spices are harvested, sun dried, and then pounded. I remember how, when I was a young girl, many ladies would come to our home and bring their pounding utensils. They would pound spices and sing so that they could work in a harmonic rhythm.

Note: Do not touch spices with your fingers. The aromas and flavors can mix with other spices and may give them different tastes. Spices do not need to be precisely measured. Use small spoons. If you want to taste a spice, try just a little at first. Many spices look alike, so experienced cooks generally identify them by smelling them at a distance of at least six inches from their noses. First learn the smell / aroma.

Store your spices in a cool, dark place in closed jars or in the refrigerator if you do not use them often. It is important to keep their containers closed so that no moisture gets inside. Do not store spices in the freezer.

Curry Leaves

Curry leaves, the flavor-enhancing leaf of the neem plant, is used mostly in western and southern India. The leaves have a special aroma, and the tree is planted in many homes that have yards because it produces shade.

The Indian name for curry leaves is "curry patta" or "neem patta." "Patta" means "leaves." Different regions have different names, but the name "neem" seems to be used the most commonly. Curry leaves are used mainly for flavoring food. There are a variety of curry plants, though. Some curry leaves are very dark green, and these plants can grow into great shade trees. There are smaller varieties with somewhat lighter green leaves, and these plants look like small fruit trees.

Both of these varieties are used to flavor soups, daals, vegetables, curry, and many other savory dishes. You can find fresh curry leaves in Indian grocery stores. When wrapped in a paper towel and stored in a plastic bag in the refrigerator, they last for quite a few days. Also, curry leaves can be dried by removing their stems and leaving them in sunny place on a plate for about three to four days. You can freeze them by coating them in oil and storing them in airtight jars.

Curry powder is not made from curry leaves.

Spice Box

Spices are the keys that unlock the special flavors and aromas of Indian cuisine. Every household in India has a spice box in the kitchen—a round or square box made up of seven containers, each of which holds one of the spices that the cook uses most often. See an example of this on the right page. This is the most common item in any Indian kitchen / household. Convenient and easy to reach, this box will prove to be your most useful tool if you want to cook Indian food. Most spice boxes contain ground cumin and coriander, turmeric powder, chili powder, whole cumin, mustard seeds, cloves, dry red chilies, and other family favorites that are used in daily food preparation.

My spice box contains whole cumin, black mustard seeds, chili powder, turmeric powder, *dhana*-jeera mix, and dry red chili (whole). An Indian kitchen is not complete without a spice box. Different regions have different styles and their own special items, and some spice boxes are made of stainless steel rather than wood. Also, each family has a special way of arranging their spice box. This book will show some simple and useful boxes and give information on how to put them together and what they should contain. Once you have experienced cooking with the basic spices in the spice box, you can experiment with new ones per the more advanced recipes.

Note: Please make sure not to touch your eyes after touching chili powder or any other spices. Do not let children touch any of the spices. It is always best to use a spoon when using spices.

Amchoor (Mango Powder)

"Aam" is a word for mango in the Hindi language. *Amchoor* is a powder that is made from dried mangoes. It is an earthy brown in color and gives a sour, tangy, and nutty taste to food. This special powder is used in many dishes from northern India, especially in Punjabi food and in spices like *chole* spice, *garam* masala, *chaat* masala, *pav bhaji* masala, etc. Many areas in India do not get fresh lemons, and lemon juice may be difficult to preserve. *Amchoor* has a very long shelf life and is easy to use. It's typically available in powder form at Indian grocery stores. This spice can form lumps in a jar, but shaking the jar will resolve this problem.

Ajwain Seeds (Ajma)

Ajwain or *carom* and anise seeds look very similar, and it is easy to mistake one for the other, but they do have different flavors tastes. Anise tastes like a mixture of licorice (*fennel*) and pepper, while *ajwain* has a more spicy taste. Since anise seeds are used in making breads, fritters, and other savory dishes, only a very small amount is necessary at a time, but they make a difference in a dish's overall flavor. *Ajwain* seeds are used in this book.

Asafetida (Hing)

Asafetida gets its name from the Persian "aza," for "mastic or resin," and the Latin "foetidus," for "stinking." It is a hard resin gum made from the sap of the roots and stem of a tree that exudes a stinking odor. It is grayish-white when fresh, darkening with age to yellow, red, and eventually brown. It is sold in blocks or pieces as a gum and more frequently as a fine yellow powder, sometimes crystalline or granulated. The smell dissipates with cooking. It is important to know that this spice has to be kept in airtight containers, as its sulfurous odor will affect other foods and spices otherwise. As a powder or granules, it can be added directly to the cooking pot. It is also sold in lumps that need to be crushed before using.

This is a very powerful spice; even in its ground state, it lasts for well over a year if stored properly, away from light and air. You will need a pinch at a time. About 1⁄16 of a teaspoon in powder form is generally added to tadka in daals and vegetables.

Basil Seeds (Takmaria) and Chia Seeds

What is the difference between chia seeds and takmaria? The main difference is that, although they are both from the mint family, they are two different species. Takmaria is a type of basil. Chia is a type of sage. The seeds of both are used in food. Recently, much has been written about the health benefits of chia seeds, but takmaria has been used for ages in Indian food. These seeds are generally soaked a teaspoon to a cup of water for 10 minutes before using. The seeds puff up in water, creating a translucent coating.

Both of these wonderful seeds can be used interchangeably in many ways: with desserts, in fruit juices, to make fruit drinks and lemonade, on ice cream or shaved ice, with syrup, on fruits, and in other sweet dishes.

Black or Brown Mustard Seeds (Raai)

In Indian cooking, brown mustard seeds are more commonly used, but black seeds contain a higher proportion of the volatile mustard oil, the strongest flavor. Both varieties are available in Indian markets. The larger yellow variety, known as white or yellow mustard, is much less pungent. Powdered mustard has some aroma when dry, but a hot taste is released when it is mixed with water. The seeds are put whole into hot oil for tadka, the tempering process. Vegetables can be cooked in this flavored oil, or it can be poured over some dishes just before serving. Ground mustard is used in salad dressing recipes to help blend oil and vinegar and add a spicy taste.

Mustard seeds are a popular addition to dishes such as vegetables, daals, and pickles. Many pickles and spreads are made with mustard powder and lemon juice or vinegar. It is important to know that, once mixed with lemon juice, mustard tends to be very hot and tangy.

Black Salt (Kala namak)

This black salt is a rock salt containing sulfur. In Hindi and Gujarati, it is called "sanchal." The raw material for producing kala namak was originally obtained from mines in northern India, Pakistan, and certain locations in the Himalayan salt ranges. The salt crystals appear black in color and are usually ground to a fine powder, which is pink. This powder is used as a spice for chaats, chutneys, pani puri, and many other savory Indian snacks. Packaged Indian snacks mostly use black salt. Chaat masala, an Indian spice blend, is dependent upon black salt for its characteristic sulfurous aroma. Those who are not accustomed to black salt often describe the smell as extremely pungent.

Cardamom (Elaichi)

Cardamom is a spice that is native to the Middle East, India, and North Africa. There are three types of cardamom: green, large brown, and white cardamom. The large brown variety is generally used whole, but it is not as soft and does not open like white or green cardamom. This variety has a mild flavor and is used in daals and other curries in northern Indian food, but it is spicy. If kept in soup or stew for a long time, it may make the dish very hot and spicy.

Ground cardamom seeds are readily available in grocery stores. It is best to buy cardamom when it is still in pods; they lose much of their flavor once they are out of the pods. Cardamom has a strong, unique, spicy-sweet taste that is slightly aromatic. Cardamom is more expensive than average spices, but a little goes a long way. If a recipe calls for 10 pods, that equals 1½ teaspoon of ground cardamom.

Cardamom lasts for a long time if it is kept in pods and closed containers. I grind the pods in a coffee grinder. The powder will contain the pod husks, but it is very flavorful. Cardamom is used in many Indian sweet dishes and in chai spice. Most recipes for four to six people will only require ¼ teaspoon of ground cardamom.

Chaat masala

Chaat masala is a mixture of spices used in Indian cuisine for flavor or garnishing spice.

Because it contains certain spices like *asafetida*, it is pungent. Once you get over the initial smell, it is sour and quite spicy. This masala typically consists of amchoor (dried mango powder), cumin, kala namak, coriander, dried ginger, salt, black pepper, asafetida, and chili powder. This spice has some Middle Eastern influence. It was introduced to India by the population in Punjab, near the border of India and Pakistan. This spice is used in dahi vada and chaat papdi, and is even sprinkled on fruits. Start out using just a pinch to sprinkle as a garnish, and then slowly add more as you get used to the taste. This spice mix is available in Indian markets.

It is best to store this spice in the refrigerator in a plastic bag so that the flavor is not lost. Chaat masala has a very long shelf life.

Chili Powder (Lal Mirch)

Important Note: After touching chili powder, do not touch your face, eyes, or any part of your body without first washing hands thoroughly. Do not let children touch this hot powder.

There are many varieties of chilies, and knowing which one to use can be confusing. Recently, many different kinds of chilies have been introduced to the world. When buying chili powder, buy it in very small quantities. Experiment per your family's tolerance, then select your favorite. You can buy many different chilies in Indian markets. The common types of Indian chili powder are *reshampatti*, (which means "silky leaves"), Kashmiri, and some "hot" and "mild" ones. It is important to select a chili powder with a bright red color. It may be very hot, so use very little at first and add more as you grow accustomed to the heat.

Make sure not to touch your eyes or any part of your body without washing your hands thoroughly after touching chili powder. Do *not* let children touch this hot powder.

Cinnamon (Dalchini)

This spice comes from the dried bark of various laurel trees in the cinnamon family. It is a sweet-tasting spice with a warm, woody aroma. The

Names of Spices in English and Hindi (in parenthesis)

Asafetida (Hing)
Basil Seeds (Tukmaria)
Bay Leaf (Tejpatta)
Black or Brown Mustard Seeds (Raai / Raee)
Black Salt (Kala Namak)
Cardamom, Brown (Elaichi Moti)
Cardamom, Green or White (Elaichi Chhoti)
Carom Seeds (Ajwain)
Chili (Mirch)
Cilantro Leaves (Dhania Patta)
Cinnamon (Dalchini)
Clarified Butter (Ghee)
Clove (Lavang)
Coriander Powder (Dhania Powder)
Cumin Powder (Jeera Powder)
Cumin Seeds (Jeera, Whole)
Curry Leaves (Neem / Limdo)
Fennel Seeds (Saunf / Variyali)
Fenugreek Seeds (Methi Akhi)
Garlic (Lasan / Lahsun)
Ginger (Adrak)
Green Chili (Hari Mirch)
Kokum (no other name)
Mace (Javitri)
Mango Powder (Amchoor)
Mint Leaves (Pudina)
Nutmeg (Jaiphal)
Pepper, Black (Kali Mirch / Gulmirch)
Saffron (Kesar)
Sesame Seeds (Til)
Star Anise (Badma)

smell of cinnamon is pleasant and stimulates the senses, yet calms the nerves. The highest-quality cinnamon has the thinnest bark. It is available as a powder as well, but is much better bought in sticks. When ground, the flavor becomes stronger. Whole cinnamon is used for spicing hot drinks. Ground cinnamon is used in some blends of spices, sweet dishes, and chai spice. Most recipes do not require more than 1/4 teaspoon of cinnamon at a time.

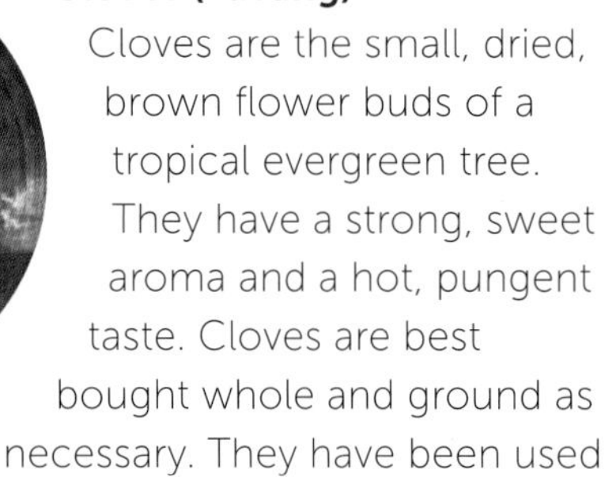

Cloves (Lavang)

Cloves are the small, dried, brown flower buds of a tropical evergreen tree. They have a strong, sweet aroma and a hot, pungent taste. Cloves are best bought whole and ground as necessary. They have been used in India for thousands of years – not only in cooking, but in sweetening the breath. They also contain a mild anesthetic. Whole cloves are frequently used to flavor meat dishes, curries, and soups. The state of Kerala grows cloves, cardamoms, and black pepper that you can buy fresh in spice stores. Cloves have been used in Ayurvedic medicine for hundreds of years. Ground cloves are used in garam masala, chai spice, and other blends.

Coriander Seeds and Powder (Dhana-Dhaniya)

Coriander is a member of the parsley family with a distinct aroma. The seeds are oval in shape, ridged, and turn from bright green to beige when ripening. This spice tastes sweet and tangy with a slightly citric flavor. Coriander is sold as seeds and in a powdered form, available in markets. Unless it is stored in the refrigerator, the shelf life of this spice is 2 to 3 months. These seeds can be planted in your garden if you want to grow fresh coriander, also known as cilantro. It grows fast and is very flavorful. Fresh green coriander / cilantro is used in daily food preparation in India and in many other countries. The Hindi word is "dhania."

Coriander powder is also used in fish and savory dishes as a healthy alternative to salt, and it is one of the basic ingredients of curry powder.

Many Indian dishes use a coriander and cumin powder mix, a blend seen in many spice boxes. This blend, *dhana-jeera*, is also available in Indian stores in already-mixed form.

Cumin seeds and Powder (Jeera)

Cumin also comes from the parsley family. The seeds are oval and ridged, with a greenish-beige color, a warm, nutty aroma, and a taste that is slightly bitter, but not hot. They can be ground to a powder. Cumin and other spices are usually dry-fried before use. Cumin is used to flavor rice, stuffed vegetables, many savory dishes, and curries. Jeera, (cumin) can be pan-roasted to bring out a strong, special aroma. You will find ground roasted jeera in almost every home in India. This roasted jeera is great to sprinkle on your plain *lassi* or chaats or as a spice for raitas, salads, and some snacks.

Coriander-cumin powder (Dhana-Jeera)

This mixture is used daily and in almost all vegetables, daals, and other dishes. To have this mixture on hand is a great convenience. This mixture is available in Indian markets. There are two varieties available — fine ground and coarse ground. The latter seem to have more flavor. Coriander and cumin powder mix is used in daily cooking in India. The Indian spice box contains dhana-jeera mix as one of its most important ingredients.

This mixture enhances the taste and flavor of daals, vegetables, and many snack dishes.

Curry Powder

Curry powder, a blend of spices that add a very strong flavor to any dish, was mainly created by cooks in India.

Dill Seeds (Suva dana)

Dill seeds look like whole cumin. However, these seeds have a spicy and nutty taste. They are used very rarely, mainly in a few specific savory dishes. I remember how, as a young girl, my mother used to give us dill water to prevent stomach problems.

Fennel Seeds (Sounf-Variyali)

Fennel is a small, green, oval-shaped seed from a plant in the parsley family. It has a sweet and licorice-like flavor. Used sparingly; it gives a warmth and sweetness to curries. Additionally, these seeds are commonly coated in colored sugar and sold in Indian markets, a very popular treat among children. They are also used in India and other countries as a mouth freshener.

Garam masala

Garam masala is a mixture/blend of spices. It can be made fresh from a family recipe or bought in a packet mix in Indian markets to save time. Recently, many U.S. markets have started carrying Indian staples like garam masala. Sold in small packets or boxes. It usually contains mustard seeds, cloves, cinnamon, dry red chilies, coriander seeds, cumin seeds, kalonji, and star anise, among other possible ingredients.

This mixture is very hot and spicy, and you may need to acquire a taste for it. Use it just a little at first.

Garam masala has a long shelf life. If you are new at it, and want to experiment with it. Add it to daals, curries, paneer tikka, and vegetables. Today many people buy packet mix to save time. The aroma of garam masala is powerful. The shelf-life of garam masala is long. Experiment with it. Use it in daals, curries, chicken tikka, paneer tikka, and vegetables. Garam masala may vary from family to family. The aroma fills the home even if only a small amount is used.

Garlic

Garlic is widely used around the world for its pungent flavor as a seasoning. The bulb is the most commonly used part of the plant. Garlic bulbs are normally divided into numerous fleshy sections called "cloves." They have

a characteristically powerful, spicy flavor that mellows and sweetens considerably with cooking.

Garlic can be peeled and stored in the freezer. It is important not to use the same knife on any other item after chopping garlic without washing it thoroughly, as garlic carries a strong smell.

Garlic powder has a different taste than fresh garlic. If it is used as a substitute, ⅛ teaspoon of garlic powder is equivalent to about one clove of garlic.

Ginger

Ginger may be the oldest spice in history. It has travelled to many countries, its name evolving from the Sanskrit word "shringarvera." It comes from a root rather than a seed, and fresh ginger is used in curries, daals, some chutneys, and many snacks. A fresh ginger and green chili paste is also common in Indian cuisine. Dry ginger, on the other hand, is a component of many spice blends. Fresh ginger can last for a few days in the refrigerator, whereas dry ginger can be stored at room temperature for quite a while. Freshly grated ginger is also a common topping in Indian cuisine.

Jaggery (Gol-gudd-gur)

Jaggery is a minimally processed and unrefined palm or cane sugar, and is used in preparing daily dishes like daals and vegetables instead of regular sugar. As a child one of my favorite treats was freshly made roti with a little ghee and sprinkled with jiggery. My children loved it and now my grandchildren love it too.

Methi (Fenugreek)

These plants grow like cilantro, small and upright. The leaves are used in making some curry and chicken dishes. The fresh leaves are bitter and have a pungent quality. It is best to use dried leaves at first in order to get used to the flavor. In many parts of India, cooks use the fresh leaves to make gourmet dishes. Fresh methi is available in Middle Eastern and Indian markets. Many cultures use fresh methi with vegetable to make soup, and methi leaves are used with daal, curry, and vegetable dishes, as well as some flatbreads. The ground methi seeds are used in an Indian pickle masala mix. Whole methi seeds are used in the tempering process to add flavor. To grow your own fresh fenugreek, plant methi seeds in the ground as you would other vegetables and pull them out or cut them as needed.

Kasoori Methi

This is a dried herb-spice. The leaves of methi (fenugreek) plants are sun dried and stored to make them last longer. The entire plant has a strong aroma, and the mature leaves have a bitter taste. Ground fenugreek seeds have a warm, yellowish-brown color with a strong, slightly bitter, curry-like taste. Powdered fenugreek is one of the ingredients in many curry powders. Fenugreek is also used to add flavor to meat dishes, and it is considered to be an aphrodisiac. Since methi has a bitter taste, it is important to practice cooking with it and understand the seasoning's effect before serving it to company.

Nigella Seeds (Kalonji)

Kalonji seeds, also known as black onion seeds, black seeds, and, most recently, nigella seeds, are generally sprinkled on breads and salads. These seeds are very similar in size to black sesame seeds, though they are slightly harder and have a different and strong aroma. Used mainly in bread recipes and savory dishes. If you love to eat Indian cuisine, then you will most likely love the flavor of the kalonji seed.

Naan breads are usually sprinkled with these seeds, so if you have eaten naan bread, you will be familiar with the taste.

Kokum

Kokum is a citrus-type fruit with the same souring qualities as lemon. It is generally used dried. You can find it dried and sliced in Indian stores. Many recipes call for kokum as a substitute for tamarind, especially to enhance coconut-based dishes and other curries or vegetable dishes and lentils / daals. Three or four slices of kokum are enough to season an average dish for four to six people, especially a daal- or vegetable-based meal. Sometimes, kokum is included in chutneys and pickles.

Licorice (Jyesthi madhu)

This root is not often used in cooking, it is a sweet tasting spice, sometimes used for sweet dishes and desserts. The licorice plant is a legume that is native to southern Europe and parts of Asia. It is unrelated to anise, star anise, or fennel. Fresh fennel tastes like licorice, but licorice is a root with similar taste. We all know about licorice in candy form, which most kids love. Licorice is used as a dried root and ground as a spice.

Mint (Foodina)

This fragrant herb is widely used in most countries. Mint is used in Indian cuisine to make sauces, chutneys and specialty dishes, as well added to tea and cool drinks. It is also used with lemon in drinking water.

Nutmeg and Mace (Jaiphal and Javitri)

Nutmeg and mace are the seed of an evergreen tree. Mace is the fleshy lattice covering of the nutmeg (hard nut), which is a golden brown in color. Although nutmeg has a more robust flavor than mace, they are otherwise very similar. The hard brown seed of the nutmeg has a warm, spicy, sweet flavor. Mace is dried lacy membrane around the nutmeg seed. It has a nutty, warm, and slightly sweet flavor. Nutmeg adds sweet and savory flavor to dishes such as vegetables, sweets, and beverages. Like nutmeg, mace is also a sweet and flavorful spice that can be substituted for nutmeg or cinnamon to complement a variety of foods. Mace is commonly used in sauces and pickled chutneys.

The first harvest of nutmeg trees takes place seven to nine years after they have been planted. The trees reach their full potential after twenty years. Nutmeg was one of the most valuable spices.

Punch Puran (five spices)

This is a popular spice-mixture of five seeds-in Eastern part of India. Seeds include fenugreek, kalonji, black mustard, fennel, and cumin in equal parts. This mixture can be used in tadka for vegetables and curries. This mixture has become more popular recently in Western region and used for potatoes, rice, and curry.

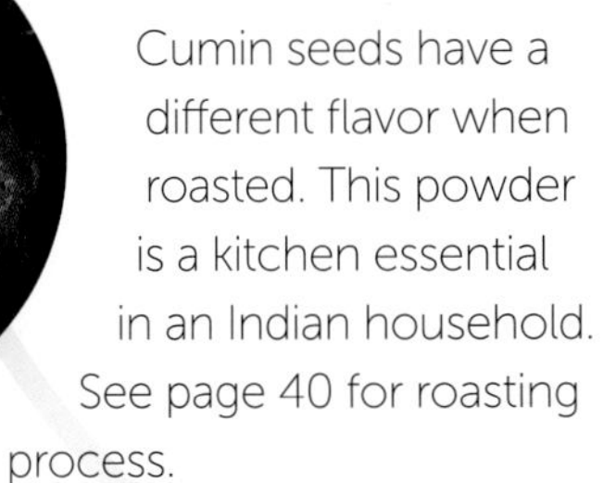

Roasted Ground Cumin (Jeera)

Cumin seeds have a different flavor when roasted. This powder is a kitchen essential in an Indian household. See page 40 for roasting process.

We did not have grinders when I was growing up. Rather, we used the stone mortar and pestle to grind seeds in small quantities. Thanks to modern gadgets, however, making roasted and ground cumin is easy. I roast it in a skillet, no oil needed. To do this, heat the skillet on a medium heat and add the seeds. Stir occasionally. This process takes only minutes, so be watchful. The seeds will start to turn brown, and you will be able to smell them. When the color of the seeds becomes slightly lighter than cocoa, turn off the heat and move the seeds to a bowl. Keeping the seeds in the hot skillet may burn them. Grind the seeds in a coffee grinder into a coarse powder, not a fine one. You can store this in a spice jar. This powder can be used with raitas, salads, lassi, kachumber, etc., and it can be combined with cloves, cinnamon, dry red chilies, coriander seeds, cumin seeds, kalonji, star anise, and more to make garam masala. This mixture is very hot and spicy, though, so you may need to acquire a taste for it. Use only a little of it at first.

Saffron (Kesar)

Saffron, grown in Spain and other countries, is the most expensive spice. It is made from the orange-colored, dried stamens of the specially cultivated crocus flower. Over seventy-five strands are needed to make one ounce of the spice. It has a distinctively pungent, honey-like sweet flavor and aroma. It is available as whole threads or a rust-colored powder. The best way to preserve saffron for a long time is to store it in an airtight, dry container. Do not use saffron while cooking. For the best result, sprinkle / mix it into a dish just after the rest of the preparation is complete. The threads can be lightly roasted, crumbled in a little hot water, and added to your dishes. When added to foods like rice, sweet dishes, and milk, saffron offers a vibrant color and aroma. Add saffron as you finish cooking and cover for best color and aroma.

Sesame Seeds

Sesame seeds are a big part of Asian cuisine. Sesame oil is used in Asian countries as well. The seeds contain oil which can be used for cooking. Seeds come in white, brown, and black varieties. They are used whole and ground and sometimes roasted. It is important to check for allergies before serving.

Star Anise (Badma)

Because of its extreme olfactory similarity to anise, star anise is named after anise.

Many countries use this flavorful spice. It is a favorite in some chai houses. The characteristically shaped fruits (pods) are always used in dried state. The essential oil resides in the outer part, not the seed. The star-shaped, dry pod has a distinct aroma, and the whole star anise pod gives great flavor to rice dishes. Like anise, star anise is warm, sweet, and aromatic.

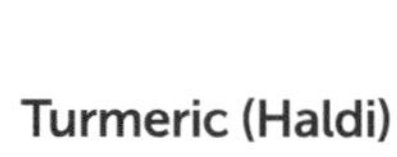

Turmeric (Haldi)

This spice is a powder made from the dry orange root of a leafy plant related to ginger. It has a bright yellow color and a warm, earthy aroma and taste, but it can become bitter if used excessively. It is also mildly antiseptic and aids digestion. Very small amounts are used in the dishes.

Turmeric is an essential spice in Indian food, giving it a rich, appetizing color. It is used in curries, daals, vegetables, and other dishes. Turmeric has a unique taste, and fresh turmeric is sometimes available in the U.S. and in Indian markets.

The pickle made from fresh turmeric is a favorite of many people from Gujarat.

Recently turmeric has been in news for its antibacterial and antihistamine properties.

Farmers used to keep turmeric powder handy for minor cuts.

Useful Weights and Measures

Dry measurements

3 teaspoons = 1 tablespoon
1 ounce = 28 grams
1 pound = 16 ounces = 454 grams
1 kilogram = 2.2 pounds
1 pinch = $\frac{1}{16}$ teaspoon = the amount you can hold between your thumb and two fingers.

Fluid measurements

1 dash = 3 drops = $\frac{1}{16}$ teaspoon
3 teaspoons = 1 tablespoon
1 pint = 2 cups
1 quart = 2 pints = 4 cups = 32 fluid ounces = 0.95 liters
1 gallon = 4 quarts = 128 fluid ounces = 3.785 liters = 3785 cubic centimeters
1 liter = 34 fluid ounces = 1.0 quart

Note: Many measurements in the recipes are "per taste," because only you know what that taste is for your palette.

Masala Recipes

These masala blends are very easy to make and last for a long time. You can keep them in tightly covered jars. I have learned, over the years, to buy a few small mason jars or preserving jars for storing spices. Grind and blend them from whole spices for the best flavor. You can also mix ready-ground spices.

Each of these masalas requires only a very small amount per use. Use very little at first if you are not accustomed to the taste. Getting the right proportion might take some practice.

I use a coffee grinder for grinding spices (and I use it only for grinding spices).

These recipes were designed for people who do not like truly spicy food, but you can make them to your preferences. *Note:* These spices may be too spicy for children.

Garam Masala

"Garam" means "hot," and "masala" means "spice." This quick recipe yields about 3 tablespoons. You can mix it in whatever way you prefer.

Ingredients:

- 2 tablespoons coriander-cumin (dhana-jeera) powder, coarsely ground
- ½ teaspoon ground cloves
- ½ teaspoon ground black pepper
- ½ teaspoon ground cinnamon

Additional Options for Northern Indian Garam Masala:

- ½ teaspoon each of ground brown and green cardamom
- 1 bay leaf, crushed

The Process:

If you are using whole spices to make this masala, roasting them for about 1 minute on a skillet will give the dish a great aroma. Cool and grind the spice mixture. Stir it well and store it. There is no need to refrigerate.

Use this masala in soups, daals, vegetables, and snack dishes to give them a spicy flavor and taste. Add this spice to a dish when you are halfway through cooking it.

Chaat Masala

Ingredients:

- 4 tablespoons amchoor powder
- 3 tablespoons roasted cumin, ground
- 1 tablespoon ground black salt
- 1 tablespoon ground black pepper

The Process:

Mix all of these ground spices together. This mixture will have a tart and salty taste. It is used for many snack dishes like bhelpuri, chaat papdi, and even as a rub on roasted vegetables or corn (after adding butter).

Nita's Special Curry Masala

Ingredients:

- ½ cup dhana-jeera (coriander-cumin) powder
- ½ teaspoon turmeric powder
- 1 tablespoon chili powder
- 1 teaspoon ginger powder
- ½ teaspoon ground cloves
- ½ teaspoon ground cinnamon

Optional:

- ½ teaspoon onion powder
- ½ teaspoon garlic powder

This recipe can be adjusted to your liking. This is a spice that you can use with vegetables, daals, a curry yogurt dip, salad dressings, and even some meat dishes.

Roasted Ground Cumin (Jeera)

Cumin seeds have a unique flavor when they are roasted. This powder is typically one of the kitchen essentials of an Indian household. We did not have grinders when I was growing up. Instead, we used stone mortars and pestles to grind the seeds as needed in small quantities. Thanks to modern gadgets, however, making jeera powder is an easy and simple process.

I roast the cumin in a skillet, no oil needed.

The Process:

Heat the skillet on medium heat. Add ¼ cup of cumin seeds and stir occasionally. This process takes only minutes, so be watchful.

The seeds will start turning brown, and you'll be able to smell their aroma. When the color of the seeds becomes slightly lighter than the color of cocoa, turn off the heat and move the seeds to a bowl. Keeping the seeds on the hot skillet may burn them.

Use a coffee grinder to grind the roasted seeds into a coarse powder, not a fine one. You can store this in a spice jar. In Indian cooking, this powder is commonly used in raitas, salads, lassi, kachumber, and to make other mixes.

Coriander-Cumin (Dhana-Jeera) Powder Mix

This mixture is used in all vegetable and daal dishes. It makes food tasty. Also, according to Ayurvedic wisdom, it helps with digestion.

This mix can be purchased at an Indian market, but it is also easy to make at home from seeds. You will need a good dry grinder.

When you buy the seeds from the market, you may have to buy more jeera than dhana. You can also use jeera in tempering. To prepare this mixture, it is important to roast these whole spices first, just a little. Do not let them change color. You will need more of this mixture than any other spice, so it is better to make a lot of it at a time.

For every 8 ounces. of dhana (coriander) seeds, you will need about 2 ounces. of jeera (cumin). Roast the seeds slightly on a flat skillet for about 5 minutes or until you can smell their aroma. They do not have to be fully roasted. This process will keep the mixture potent for a long time. Grind it when it cools, and store the powder in an airtight jar. It can last for almost a year.

Achar Masala

This recipe requires coarse ground methi (also known as "methi kuria") and split mustard, also known as "rai kuria." Both are available in Indian markets. This mustard will be yellow without any black color. You can adjust the chili powder and the other ingredients to your taste once you have an idea of what grade of spiciness you like. The masala will be slightly oily.

This recipe makes about 1½ cups. This masala can be used on raw mangoes, carrots, or bell peppers. It can be kept for a few months in a glass jar.

You will need to use a tablespoon for about 1 cup of raw mango.

Ingredients:

- ½ cup chili powder
- ½ cup coarse ground methi
- ¼ cup coarse ground mustard seeds
- ¼ to ½ cup salt, or per taste
- ¼ cup oil
- ¼ teaspoon asafetida (optional: check for allergies)

The Process:

Mix all of the ingredients in a large bowl using a spoon — no hands, please. This spice is salty and a bit oily and may taste slightly bitter, but it preserves the achar masala.

Nita's Kachumber Masala

This is a mixture of spices used for kachumber, and these items are already in the kachumber recipes.

Having this mixture handy may save you time as you do not have to look for each item when you make kachumber.

You can alter the amount according to your taste. Sugar is used to cut the tanginess and hot taste.

This recipe makes about ¼ cup of spice mixture. Put this in to a jar and use about ¼ teaspoon (or per taste) for 2 cups of kachumber.

This spice keeps good for 3 to 4 months – do not refrigerate.

Ingredients

- 1 tablespoon salt
- 3 tablespoons roasted ground cumin
- 2 tablespoons of ground black pepper
- ½ teaspoon of citric acid crystals
- 1 teaspoon raw sugar

If you prefer a little more spicy, add about ½ teaspoon of chili powder to the mixture.

Kachumber masala.

Achars, Chutneys, Raita, and Kachumber

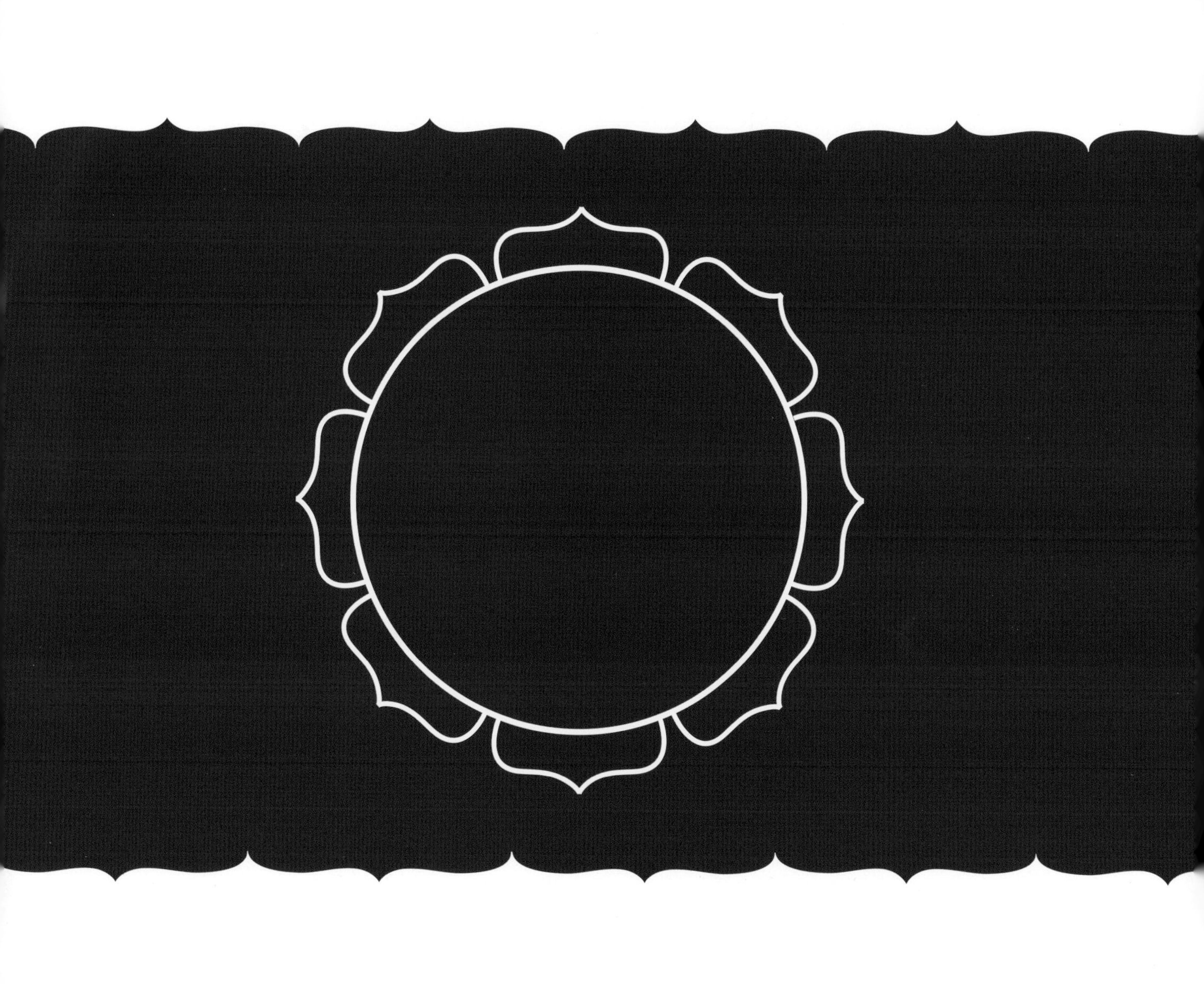

Achars, Chutneys, Raita, and Kachumber

SAUCES, SALADS, AND CONDIMENTS

Trays of achars or chutneys – condiments, pickles, or relishes that are used to flavor or complement food — accompany all meals in India. Many of these achars are made fresh, and the recipes vary from region to region and family to family. Some achars are prepared in advance for the whole year using green mangoes or other seasonal fruits and vegetables and are either salted, or doused with sugar and sun dried, or cooked until they are ready to be stored. Many pickle, relish, and achar spice mixes are available in Indian grocery stores. *Note:* When eating an achar, it is important to take just a little at a time with a piece of roti or bread.

Chutneys are like salsas, and they are sometimes used as dipping sauces. The main ingredients are different depending on the chutney's type. Chutneys are traditionally made fresh daily in Indian homes, but now, with the convenience of refrigerators, chutneys can be kept fresh for up to 4 days at a time. Green chutneys are very diverse. Green chutneys can be used as sandwich spreads, sauces, or dips. Additionally, they can be used to add flavor and a spicy taste to daals, vegetables, and other savory items. Once you know what kind of taste a chutney will add to a dish, you can create many delicious items.

In most regions of India, at least one meal per day contains a yogurt dish, since yogurt is a primary source of calcium. Raita is a wonderful yogurt creation that uses vegetables, fruits, and other healthy ingredients. It is made with plain, low-fat yogurt or Greek-style yogurt, which is a little thicker in consistency and will need to be diluted with milk or water. Raita can be a great side dish, especially if your main dish is hot and spicy, since it cools the palate.

Kachumbers, finally, are dishes that are made with fresh vegetables like cucumbers, cabbages, tomatoes, bell peppers, and sweet peppers. A kachumber is served as a condiment, not as a bowl of salad. There is no dressing used, but most kachumbers are flavored with salt, black pepper, cumin, and fresh lemon juice. Most kachumbers will also include onions, but this depends on the preference of the family.

Recipes in This Chapter

Achars – Spicy Condiments

Kachumbers – Fresh Vegetables

Chutneys – Paste or Salsa-Style Condiments

Raitas – Yogurt-Based Dishes

Utensils Needed

To make chutney, it would be ideal to use a blender / grinder or a food processor.

While preparing any dish or a recipe, it can be very helpful to have prep bowls, a pan to boil water in, measuring cups and spoons, other spoons, knives, a chopping board, and a whisk to stir or blend yogurt. If you plan to store your achars, remember to keep some jars ready.

ACHARS

KACHUMBERS

CHUTNEYS

RAITAS

Colorful Pepper and Carrot Achar 

This is a tasty and colorful alternative to green chutney, since it uses red, yellow, or orange bell peppers. This dish is a relish, not a chutney. This dish goes well with naan, rice, or any meal that needs a spicy condiment.

Utensils:

- A medium-sized pan or skillet
- A chopping board and a knife
- A wooden spoon
- A serving bowl
- Measuring cups and spoons

Ingredients:

- 1 each of red, yellow, and orange bell peppers or 9 colorful sweet peppers (Remove seeds and cut into 1-inch pieces)
- 2 to 3 carrots, cut lengthwise and sliced
- 2 tablespoons ground peanuts or 1 tablespoon grated coconut (Use coconut in the case of a peanut allergy.)
- ½ teaspoon chili powder
- 1 teaspoon salt (or to taste)
- 1 tablespoon coriander-cumin powder
- ¼ teaspoon turmeric powder
- 1 tablespoon lemon juice (for serving)

For Tadka:

- 2 tablespoons cooking oil
- ¼ teaspoon cumin seeds
- ¼ teaspoon mustard seeds

The Process:

In a pan, heat the oil for about ½ minute, keeping a watchful eye on it. Once the oil is hot, add the cumin and mustard seeds. When the seeds crackle and become fragrant, add the peppers, carrots, and chili.

Cook for about 2 to 3 minutes.

Add the salt, coriander-cumin powder, turmeric, and peanuts (or coconut). Cook at a low heat, without stirring, for about 3 minutes. The vegetables should be slightly wilted at the end of this step, but still somewhat crisp.

Remove the pan from the heat source. Stir in the lemon juice just before serving.

Green Chili Achar with Chickpea Flour 

This achar is generally made fresh just before serving. You can use any kind of chili, but Thai chilies (which are very mild) work best. This recipe requires chickpea flour and achar spice, which are both available at Indian markets. ***Caution:*** Be very careful when using the chilies.

Utensils:

- A small nonstick skillet
- A chopping board and a knife
- A spatula or spoon to stir
- Measuring cups and spoons
- Bowls

Ingredients:

- About 6 to 8 green chilies with the seeds removed, cut lengthwise and then sliced into ½-inch pieces.(Keep them in a bowl of water.)
- ¼ cup chickpea flour
- 2 tablespoons achar spice
- ½ teaspoon salt
- 1 tablespoon coriander-cumin powder
- ¼ teaspoon sugar
- ½ teaspoon lemon juice or a small slice of lime or lemon
- 3 tablespoons cooking oil
- ¼ teaspoon each black mustard and cumin seeds

The Process:

Heat the oil. It takes about ½ minute. Add the black mustard and cumin seeds. When they start splattering, take the skillet off the heat and add the drained chilies. Put the pan back on the stove and stir it a little. Add the salt and cook for two more minutes at a low heat.

Mix the chickpea flour, achar spice, coriander-cumin powder, and sugar and gently add this to the chilies. Stir the mixture in gently until it has no lumps. You may need to add a little oil, as the chickpea flour absorbs it.

Cook for about a minute, then take the pan off of the heat. Do not cover, as this may alter the color of the chilies. Add the lemon juice just before serving.

Fresh Raw Mango Achar 

This is a seasonal achar, since mangoes are a seasonal fruit. The raw green ones are a special kind, different from the ripe ones. These mangoes have a lot of pulp.

The mango that is used must be really raw, green, and firm. Raw mango is tart and may not suit everyone's tastes.

This recipe uses achar mix, which is available in Indian markets, and will keep well for days in the refrigerator. This achar requires a lot of oil to preserve it, but you do not need to consume this oil, as it is very spicy. To serve, just scoop out the achar without the oil.

Utensils:

- A chopping board and knife
- A tadka pot
- Measuring spoons and cups
- 2 or 3 bowls
- Measuring spoons
- A storage container

Ingredients:

- 1 raw green mango, peeled and diced. Wash and drain it and keep it in a large bowl.
- 2 teaspoons achar mix
- 3 tablespoons cooking oil
- 1 tablespoon coriander-cumin powder
- ¼ teaspoon salt (or to taste)
- ½ teaspoon chili powder
- ½ teaspoon whole fennel
- ¼ teaspoon black mustard
- ¼ teaspoon whole cumin

The Process:

In the large bowl of mango, add the salt, achar mix, coriander-cumin powder, chili powder, and fennel. Mix so that the spices coat the mango pieces.

Heat cooking oil in the tadka pot. Add the dry seeds after about ½ minute when the oil is slightly hot. The seeds will crackle. Pour this oil over the mango mixture. Let it sit for a minute and mix. Depending on which spices you like, you can add more and stir.

More oil may be needed before storing the dish in a jar. This is a pickle that should be well oiled.

Store in the refrigerator and eat with roti and other meals as a condiment. This will last for 10 days.

Carrot and Jalapeño Achar 

This condiment can be prepared very quickly. It can be very spicy, but you can use green bell peppers instead of jalapeños if you want to make it milder. This achar can be kept in the refrigerator for about 7 to 10 days.

Utensils:

- A tadka pot
- A spoon to mix the achar
- A chopping board and a knife
- A mixing bowl
- Measuring cups and spoons

Ingredients:

- 2 to 3 jalapeño peppers, remove seeds, chopped
- 3 to 4 carrots, peeled, cut lengthwise in to 2-inch pieces, then make about 1/4 inch long slices
- 2 tablespoons achar spice mix (available in Indian markets)
- 3 tablespoon cooking oil
- 1/2 teaspoon panch puran mix (also called "panch phoron")
- 1 tablespoon coriander-cumin powder
- 1/2 teaspoon salt
- 1/4 teaspoon sugar
- 1/2 teaspoon citric acid (This is crystalized and used in preserving food; it will give the dish a tangy taste)
- 1 tablespoon achar masala (optional)
- 4 curry leaves

The Process:

Slice the jalapeño peppers in half lengthwise, remove their seeds, and then cut them into about 1/2-inch to 1-inch pieces. Keep them in water.

Peel and cut the carrots lengthwise and slice them to about 1/4-inch thick pieces. Keep them in water.

Drain the jalapeños and carrots just before heating the oil. Put the drained peppers and carrots in a large bowl and mix them together. Add the achar spice, coriander-cumin powder, salt, sugar, and citric acid.

Heat the oil in your tadka pot at medium-low heat for no more than 1/2 minute. Add the panch puran spice. Once you can hear the seeds crackle and see that their color has changed, add the curry leaves and pour the hot oil over the peppers and carrots.

Mix gently until all of the peppers and carrots have been coated well. You may need a little more oil.

Once the achar is cool, store it in a mason or other type of jar. *Note:* Make sure that there is enough oil in the jar to totally cover the achar. This dish goes well with naan, roti, rice, or any meal that needs a spicy condiment.

Colorful Kachumber Salad 

Generally, no oil or vinegar is used for the salad dressing. The idea is to use ingredients that you like and make the dish colorful. Mix the spices in just before serving. The most common ingredients for the dressing are salt, lemon juice, chili powder, roasted cumin powder, black pepper, a little sugar, and green chilies (if you like the dressing to be spicy). The most commonly used vegetables are cabbages, radishes, carrots, cucumbers, any color of bell peppers, jicama, and green or purple onions. However you make this dish, it will be vibrant, healthy, and tasty.

Utensils:

- A chopping board
- A knife
- Measuring cups and spoons
- Tongs for mixing the ingredients

Ingredients:

- 1 cup finely chopped green cabbage
- 2 Middle Eastern cucumbers (5 to 6 inches long), cut lengthwise and then sliced into half rounds
- 6 radishes, sliced and halved
- ¼ purple onion, diced
- 1 4-inch piece of carrot, shredded
- 1 apple, cubed
- 1 avocado, peeled and cubed
- 1 firm tomato, cubed
- 2 tablespoons chopped cilantro

Dressing:

- 1 teaspoon salt (or to taste)
- ½ teaspoon black pepper
- ¼ to ½ teaspoon chili powder (optional)
- ½ to 1 teaspoon roasted cumin powder
- 2 teaspoons lemon juice (or to taste)

The Process:

Mix all of the vegetables except tomato into the serving bowl.

Add the dressing spices and cilantro. Top the mixture with the sliced tomatoes, toss it, and serve.

Fruit and Vegetable Kachumber 

This kachumber goes great with any meal. I used some fruits and other vegetables I had in the refrigerator.

Utensils:

- A chopping board and knife
- Bowls to prepare items
- Measuring cups and spoons
- A serving bowl
- A serving spoon

Ingredients:

- 2 stalks celery, strings removed and sliced ¼ inch thick
- 1 firm kiwi fruit, peeled and cut into four pieces lengthwise, then sliced
- 1 small cucumber, cut lengthwise and sliced into pieces ½ inch thick
- 1 firm apple, cubed (A Fiji apple or another variety of pink apple works well)
- ½ cup baby spinach, hand cut into small pieces
- ¼ cup each of red grapes and blueberries, washed
- 2 each of sweet red and yellow peppers, cut in ½-inch pieces
- Spinach leaves to line the serving bowl
- ¼ teaspoon salt
- ½ teaspoon lemon juice
- ¼ teaspoon roasted ground cumin or chili powder (optional)
- Ground black pepper to sprinkle

The Process:

Put all cut fruits and vegetables in a bowl and gently mix them. Line the serving bowl with spinach leaves on the side and gently arrange fruits and vegetables in the bowl without disturbing the spinach.

Add spices and lemon juice before serving.

Kachumber with Sprouted Mung (V)

Generally I make a kachumber with what I have in the refrigerator and sometimes use sprouted beans from the freezer. I put them in the hot water before using.

Utensils:

- A chopping board and knife
- Bowls to prepare items
- Measuring cups and spoons
- A serving bowl
- A serving spoon

Ingredients:

- 2 cups chopped cabbage
- ½ cup chopped purple cabbage
- 4 to 5 radishes, partially peeled and sliced
- ½ each of red and yellow bell peppers with their seeds removed, sliced
- ¼ cup sprouted mung
- ½ teaspoon sugar
- ¼ teaspoon salt
- ½ teaspoon lemon juice

The Process:

Mix the cabbages, radishes, and peppers together. Add sugar and top with the sprouted mung. Add the salt, pepper, and lemon juice before serving. Mix and serve.

Kachumber for All Seasons 

This dish is best served with meals during the season when cranberries are available in the market. It can also be served as a pickle, and it needs tadka and hot oil. A tadka pot is a necessary utensil for this dish.

Utensils:

- A chopping board and knife
- Bowls to prepare items
- Measuring cups and spoons
- A serving bowl
- A serving spoon

Ingredients:

- 2 carrots, peeled, cut lengthwise, and sliced
- 1 each of green, red, yellow, and orange bell peppers, cut into ½-inch pieces
- 6 radishes, cut into ½-inch slices
- ¼ cup pomegranate seedlings (if available)
- ½ teaspoon sugar
- ½ teaspoon salt

For Tadka:

- ½ teaspoon each black mustard seeds and cumin seeds
- 1 teaspoon sesame seeds
- 1 teaspoon oil

The Process:

Mix all ingredients in a mixing bowl mix gently so sugar has melted somewhat.

Heat the oil in tadka pot. Add the mustard and cumin seeds. When they crackle, turn off heat source and add the sesame seeds. Wait for a minute — till sesame seeds turn color.

Add the tadka mixture to the vegetables. Mix and serve.

Green Chutney 

This is a very versatile chutney. You can use it as a sandwich spread, add it to yogurt or sour cream to make a dip, or use it as a sauce with pakoras and many other snacks, like papdi chaat and bhelpuri. You can add it to daal and vegetables if you do not have ginger-chili paste. It can even give your soups a little spice. Adding tomatoes, cucumber, and lettuce makes a very healthy salad sandwich, also called "a Bombay Sandwich." For variation, you can use some mint as well and make mint chutney. Makes about 1 cup.

Utensils:

- A food processor
- Mixing bowls
- A chopping board and a good knife
- A storage jar

Ingredients:

- 2 cups cups cilantro (directions in recipe)
- 2 jalapeño or serrano chilies (or any available). You may use less or more as desired.
- 1½ inch fresh ginger, peeled and chopped
- 1½ teaspoon sugar
- ½ teaspoon salt
- 1 tablespoon coriander-cumin or dhana jeera powder mix
- ¼ cup grated coconut
- ¼ cup dalia or crushed corn chips
- 2 tablespoons lemon juice
- (1/4) cup chopped mint (optional – for mint chutney)

The Process:

Soak the cilantro in cold water to clean it. Drain the cilantro in a colander, dry it on a paper towel, and roughly chop it.

Put all of the ingredients into the blender, with the larger items going in first. Blend until the mixture turns into a non-lumpy paste. You may have to pause and check its progress multiple times.

Store the chutney in an airtight jar. This chutney can be stored in the refrigerator for 3 to 5 days and in the freezer for up to 3 months. You can also store it in small jars and take them out of the freezer as needed.

Date and Tamarind Chutney 

This chutney probably takes longer to prepare than a chutney with fresh ingredients. The pitted dates and tamarinds with the dry skin removed must be soaked and boiled separately. If you cannot find tamarind, you can buy tamarind pulp in a jar or a tube, which is typically available at Indian markets. Using 1 cup of dates and 2 tablespoons of tamarind pulp will make close to 3 to 4 cups of chutney. This chutney can be prepared days ahead of time and be stored in the freezer until you want to use it.

Utensils:

- A good blender
- A pan to soak and boil the dates
- Mixing bowls
- Measuring cups and spoons
- A storage container

Ingredients:

- 1 cup pitted dates + 3 cups of water, to rinse and soak overnight (Baking dates are used for the same purpose. Soak for half an hour and you can use it without boiling.)
- 2-3 cups of water to boil the dates
- 2 tablespoons tamarind pulp from store-bought jar + ½ cup water
- 2 tablespoons or less of sugar. (Taste after adding one tablespoon and add more as needed)
- 1 tablespoon ground coriander-cumin mix
- ½ teaspoon salt
- ½ teaspoon chaat masala
- ½ teaspoon chili powder (if you like it spicy)

The Process:

Soak the dates overnight in the water. In the morning, crush the dates gently with your hands and check that there are no hard pits in them, then bring them to a boil. Turn down the heat and let them simmer for about 10 minutes after the water reaches boiling.

Turn off the heat and let the dates cool, then put them in the blender. Make sure that there are no seeds and hard ends in them. Blend them and make a puree. You may have to add about ½ to 1 cup of water.

Add all of the spices and the tamarind pulp. Blend well until the puree is a smooth paste. This must look like a thick batter.

Tomato Chutney 

This chutney makes a great curry base. Tadka with urad dal, oil, and cumin can be used to give it a nutty taste, but these are optional. *Special item needed:* dalia — you can substitute this with corn chips if necessary.

Utensils:

- A blender
- A tadka pot for tempering
- Mixing bowls
- Measuring cups and spoons

Ingredients:

- 2 to 3 tomatoes, cut into ½-inch cubes
- 4 oz. (about ½ small can or 4 tablespoons) of tomato paste. (Use the canned variety without salt to give a nice red color to the chutney)
- ½ cup dalia. (Substitute with crushed corn chips if dalia is not available)
- 1 medium-sized white or yellow onion, chopped
- 1 teaspoon garlic, crushed
- ½ to 1 teaspoon salt (to taste)
- 2 tablespoons or less red chili powder
- 1 teaspoon sugar
- 1 tablespoon coriander-cumin powder
- ½ to 1 cup water
- 1 tablespoon cooking oil
- ½ teaspoon cumin, whole
- 4 to 5 curry leaves
- ½ teaspoon split urad dal (Optional — urad dal gives this chutney a slightly nutty taste)

The Process:

Put water, tomatoes, tomato paste, and onions into a pan and bring them to a boil. Boil for about 3 minutes, then cool. Add the coriander-cumin, chili powder, garlic, dalia, salt, and sugar, then put this mixture into a blender and blend until it becomes thick like a salsa, smooth rather than chunky.

Heat oil in a pan for about ½ minute. Add urad dal and cook until it turns color. Add the curry leaves and turn off the heat. Pour this oil into the mixture in the blender and blend it all a little more.

Check for taste in case you want to add more salt or sugar. You can store this chutney in a jar in the refrigerator for about 4 to 5 days or in the freezer for about 3 to 4 months.

Coconut Chutney

This chutney is popular with South Indian dishes such as dosa and idli. Also, if you like coconut, it can be served as a dip or a spread just by adding a little more yogurt.

Special Items Needed:

- dalia or roasted, split chickpeas; curry leaves, which are available in Indian markets; split urad dal, which gives the chutney a nutty flavor.

Utensils:

- A blender
- A tadka pot for tempering
- Mixing bowls
- Measuring cups and spoons

Ingredients:

- 1 cup grated coconut
- 1 cup dalia or roasted, split chickpeas
- 1 cup chopped cilantro
- 1 to 2 whole jalapeño or serrano chilies, cut into ½-inch pieces (You can use any green chili that is available and measure it according to how much spice you want in the dish)
- ½ teaspoon salt
- 1 cup yogurt

The Process:

Put these items into a blender and blend until they are somewhat coarse, but pasty. Add more yogurt or a bit of water if the chutney grinds and becomes hard like a dough. The consistency should be like a thick, pasty salsa.

For Tadka-Tempering:

1 tablespoon cooking oil
1 teaspoon urad dal
½ teaspoon black mustard seeds
About 4 curry leaves

The Process:

Heat the cooking oil in a small pot for about half to one minute. It would be useful to have a tadka pot, but if you don't, just use a smallest pot you have.

Add the urad dal. Let it simmer in the oil until it starts to turn color. Turn off the heat and add the black mustard seeds and curry leaves. If the leaves are fresh, the oil may splatter, so be careful.

Now add this oil mixture to the chutney. Garnish with some cilantro and serve.

Garlic Chutney 

Unlike other chutneys, which are like sauces, this chutney is dry and can be made into a ball. That is what people in Indian villages do in order to save it for days. Farmers generally take this chutney with them for lunch, along with rotla and a chaash yogurt drink. This recipe is hot, and it can be used to give a little spicy taste to a meal. In Indian villages, the women traditionally use grinding stones to make this chutney. You can make it in a blender or a small grinder, then add water to grind or blend it into a paste. This chutney can be eaten with bhelpuri and many other savory items. Add a little dried coconut if it comes out too soft. You can also add just a little of this chutney to daal or vegetables to give them a great spiciness.

Utensils:

- A blender
- Measuring cups and spoons
- Mixing bowls
- A storage container

Ingredients:

- 1 bulb garlic, cut into small pieces
- 5 tablespoons coriander-cumin powder
- 2 tablespoons red chili powder
- 2 tablespoons cooking oil
- ½ to 1 teaspoon salt (or to taste)
- 1 tablespoon lemon juice

The Process:

Put all of the items into a grinder until a thick paste is formed. You may need to add a little more liquid at this point.

Scrape this paste into a jar and save it in the refrigerator. This chutney can be stored in the refrigerator for months.

Cucumber Raita

This raita is typically served in restaurants in many Western countries. It is simple to prepare, and you can make it two different ways: You can either dice the cucumbers, or shred them. Remember to squeeze the juice out of the cucumbers if you shred them and add salt when you serve. This raita can be made ahead of time and lasts for up to 3 days in the refrigerator. Raitas are considered to be a side dish, and a single serving is about ½ cup makes about 3 cups and serves 4 to 6.

Utensils:

- 2 or 3 mixing bowls
- 2 or 3 small bowls
- A whisk and spoons
- A bowl for serving
- A chopping board and a knife
- Measuring cups and spoons
- A shredder

Ingredients:

- 2 cups cucumber, diced or shredded (Lebanese/Middle Eastern cucumbers work best for this recipe. There is no need to peel them. If you are shredding the cucumbers, use 3 to 4 of them and squeeze out the juice)
- 2 cups plain yogurt
- ½ to 1 teaspoon salt, to add when serving
- ½ teaspoon sugar
- 1 teaspoon cumin seeds, roasted and crushed (Half of these will be mixed into the dish, and half will be sprinkled on top)
- 1 teaspoon or less of black pepper
- ½ teaspoon paprika
- 2 teaspoons chopped cilantro
- ¼ green chili, finely chopped (optional)

The Process:

Roast the cumin seeds on a dry pan over medium heat until they become darker and fragrant. When cool, place them in a mortar bowl and crush with a pestle until they become a coarse powder. You can also make this spice ahead of time and store it in a jar.

In a mixing bowl, whisk together the yogurt with the sugar, half of the roasted and crushed cumin seeds, and the black pepper. Stir in the chopped cucumber.

Just before serving, add the salt, 1 teaspoon of cilantro, and the green chili and stir. Garnish with the remaining roasted and crushed cumin seeds, the remaining cilantro, and the paprika.

Boondi Raita

This raita is very popular in northern India. Boondi is a dish made of savory, salted, crispy balls that have been previously cooked or fried. Even children may like to eat them directly from the package. The boondi will puff and soften when placed in a yogurt mix.

It is best to buy boondi in an Indian market. There are two varieties available: plain and spicy. If you are trying this recipe for the first time, it will be better to buy the plain variety. The plastic packages are available in two sizes. Buy the small one at first. The Northern Indian variety of this dish has mustard, but it ferments. I have not used mustard in this recipe. This mixture can be made a few hours ahead of serving. The whole process of this recipe will take about 10 minutes.

Utensils:

- A whisk
- 3 bowls (2 for prep work, 1 to serve)
- Measuring cups and spoons
- A chopping board and a knife

Ingredients:

- 2 cups + 2 teaspoons boondi (to use as a garnish)
- 2 cups plain, low-fat yogurt
- ½ cup plain, low-fat milk
- ½ teaspoon salt
- ½ teaspoon sugar
- 2 teaspoons chopped cilantro / coriander leaves
- 1 teaspoon roasted ground cumin
- ¼ teaspoon chili powder or paprika (if making a mild raita, add more to taste)
- ½ chili, chopped (optional)

The Process:

First, put the boondi in the milk. In the meantime, whisk the yogurt in another bowl and add the salt, sugar, and half of the roasted cumin powder.

Add the boondi with milk to this mixture. Stir it in very gently. Pour this raita gently into the serving bowl.

You can keep it in the refrigerator for a few hours before serving.

Garnish with cilantro / coriander, roasted cumin, paprika, and extra boondi, then serve.

Carrot and Corn Raita

This is great raita to serve during the fall season. The oranges and yellows, when mixed with some pomegranate seeds and boondi, make this dish very colorful and eye-catching. Almost all raitas are made in a similar way. Once you know what amount of each ingredient to use according to your tastes, they will be very easy and healthy dishes to make. I have used frozen white corn in the recipe. You can use yellow corn if you like. Whatever variety you use, though, just make sure that the corn is fully cooked. You can use leftover corn as well. This recipe serves 4 to 6 people and produces about 3½ cups.

Utensils:

- A whisk
- 3 to 4 bowls for preparation
- Measuring cups and spoons
- A chopping board and a knife
- Shredder
- Chopping gadget for nuts

Ingredients:

- 1 cup frozen, boiled, and cooled white corn
- 1 cup shredded carrots
- 1½ cups plain yogurt
- ¼ cup milk
- ½ teaspoon salt or more (to taste)
- ½ teaspoon sugar
- 1 tablespoon cooking oil
- ½ teaspoon whole cumin
- ½ teaspoon black mustard
- 4 to 5 curry leaves
- ½ teaspoon split urad dal

For the Garnish:

- ¼ cup boondi
- ¼ cup pomegranate seeds
- 1 tablespoon chopped cilantro
- ½ teaspoon roasted ground cumin

The Process:

First, boil the corn. In the meantime, shred the carrots. Whisk the yogurt and milk together in a large bowl. Add the boiled, cooled corn, then add the salt and sugar.

Heat the oil in a skillet for about ½ minute. Add the urad dal, whole cumin, black mustard, and curry leaves. Turn off the heat and add the carrots. Let this mixture sit for about 5 minutes.

Gently add the carrot mixture to the yogurt and corn. Garnish with the pomegranate seeds and cilantro. Add the boondi last in order to make the raita crispy.

This raita can be kept in the refrigerator for up to 3 to 4 hours before serving. If you stir gently when serving, the bright orange color will spread. Any leftovers can be kept in the refrigerator for 2 to 3 days.

Mixed Vegetable Raita

If you are tired of serving cooked vegetables, this is a wonderful alternative. In the summer, this raita is delicious as a part of a cool lunch salad. You can make this recipe a few hours ahead of serving, if necessary. This recipe makes about 4 cups and serves 4 to 6 people. It can also be doubled, if needed.

Utensils:

- A whisk
- 3 to 4 bowls for preparation
- Measuring cups and spoons
- A chopping board and a knife
- Shredder
- Chopping gadget for nuts

Ingredients:

- ½ cup finely shredded purple cabbage
- ½ cup finely shredded green cabbage
- ½ cup shredded carrots
- ½ cup diced cucumbers (The small, Middle Eastern variety works best)
- 1½ cup yogurt
- ½ cup boondi
- 1 tablespoon chopped cilantro / coriander leaves
- ½ teaspoon salt (or to taste)
- ½ teaspoon sugar
- 1 teaspoon roasted ground cumin

The Process:

Mix the vegetables and set them aside.

Whisk the yogurt, salt, sugar, and half of the roasted ground cumin together in a large bowl, then add the vegetables. Blend this mixture with a spoon and garnish with cilantro.

Mix again before serving, adding the boondi and remaining roasted cumin powder. The boondi will absorb some liquid.

Royal Raita

This raita is made up of healthy and tasty vegetables, fruits, nuts, and crispy boondi for a garnish. It is very colorful and has many textures, with a wonderful crunchy taste. This recipe can also be served as a healthy dessert. You can add or remove items if you are allergic or do not want them. This recipe serves 6 to 8 people and makes about 4 cups.

Utensils:

- A whisk
- 3 to 4 bowls for preparation
- Measuring cups and spoons
- A chopping board and a knife
- Shredder
- Chopping gadget for nuts

Ingredients:

- 2 cups plain, low-fat yogurt
- About ½ cup plain milk
- 1 cup shredded cucumber
- About ½ cup each (depending on availability) of:
  - Fresh-washed grapes
  - Diced strawberries
  - Apple, pear, peach, or any other firm fruit you like, diced
  - Blueberries
- About ¼ cup each of chopped almonds, cashews, golden raisins, and dried cranberries
- ½ cup boondi
- ½ teaspoon chopped cilantro (for garnish)
- ½ teaspoon salt (or to taste)
- ½ teaspoon sugar
- ½ teaspoon black pepper powder (if desired)

The Process:

Whisk the yogurt with the salt and sugar until it is smooth. You may need to add some milk so that this mixture is not very thick.

Add all of the other ingredients except the boondi and cilantro, and gently mix this until everything is

coated with yogurt. Top this mixture with the saved fruit and nuts. Garnish with boondi and cilantro (optional).

This dish can be prepared a few hours before serving. Add the saved fruits, nuts, cilantro, and boondi directly before serving.

Roti, Parathas, Bhakri, and Puris

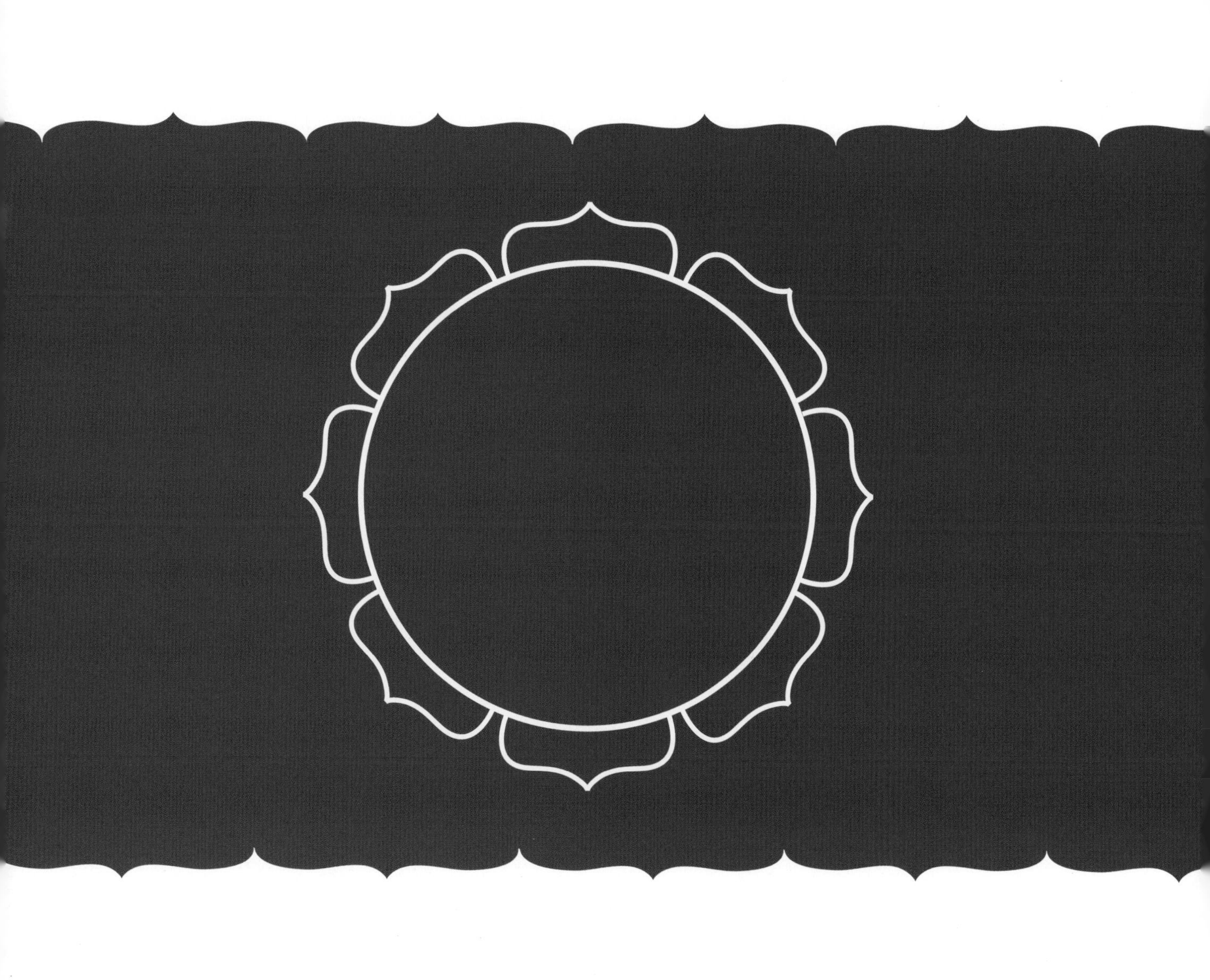

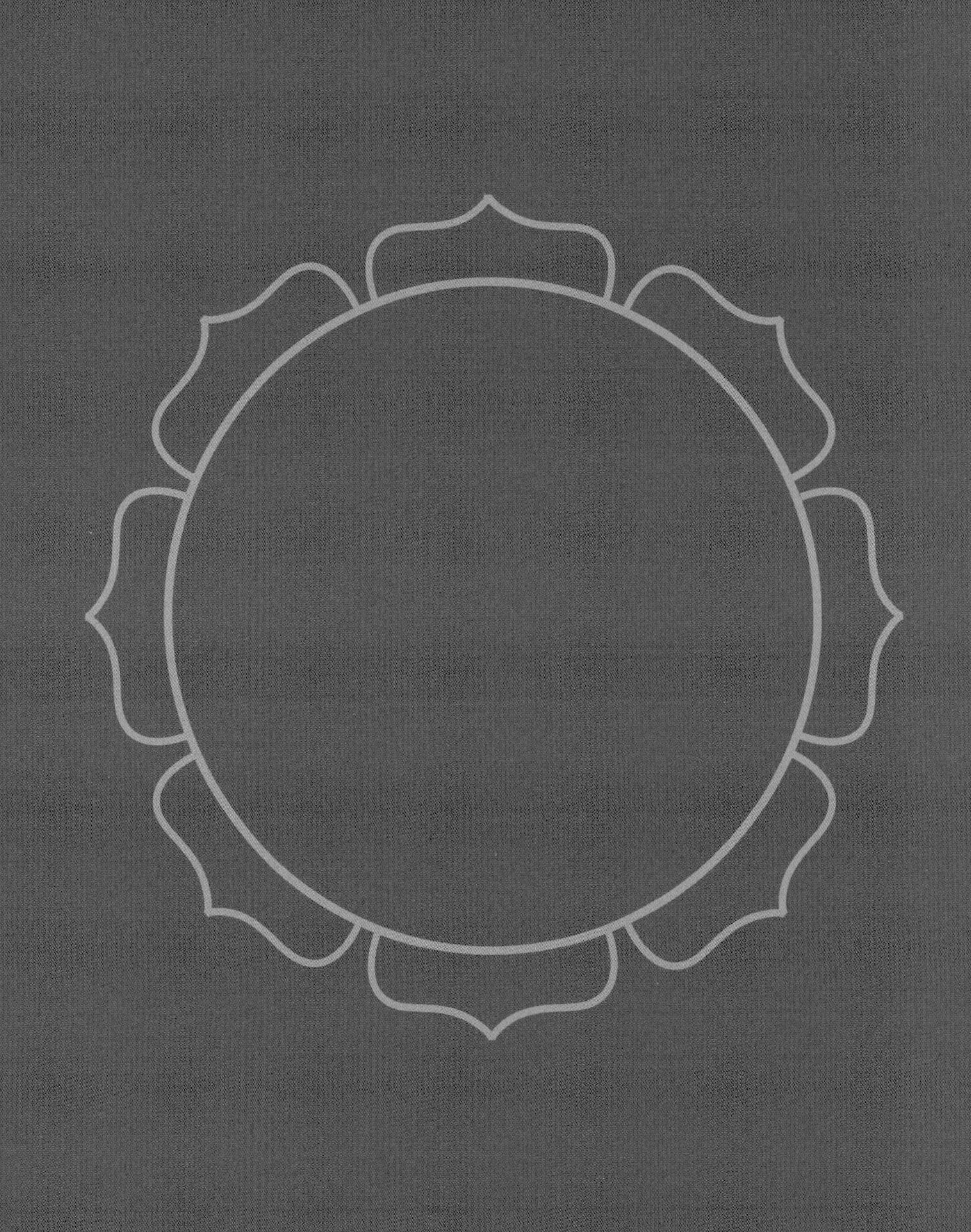

Roti, Parathas, Bhakri, and Puris

FLATBREADS

"Roti" means "bread," and rotis come in several popular and delicious varieties in India. Soft, tasty and sometimes colorful, they are also utilitarian, used by Indians to scoop up vegetables, daal, rice, and other items on the dinner plate. They are often served with yogurt or raita and chutneys to make a full meal. Making Indian bread is an art and a very creative process.

Important Note: The breads in this section are made from whole wheat flour. The whole wheat flour that is available in regular local supermarkets may contain bran or may be ground coarsely, which will not give you the correct texture and softness. Indian markets have many varieties of chapatti flour, including a multigrain version that is available in 5-pound+ packages. Store this in the refrigerator to keep it from spoiling, unless you use it often. Naan bread, unlike roti bread, is made from white flour.

The chapatti (flatbread) looks a little like a tortilla, but is softer and can be made from wheat or multigrain flour. Breads made from millet are little thicker and do not need a leavening agent. Plain chapattis are made fresh every day in Indian kitchens and devoured by the young and old alike. A growing youngster usually consumes as many as 4 to 6 chapattis per meal. To make these breads, you do not need to sift the flour, and no leavening or baking is required.

Indian flatbreads are versatile, as they can be used to scoop vegetables, daal, or any food off a plate (though most Indians now use spoons or forks with their meals). You can make rolls out of these breads with vegetables, salads, peanut butter, or cutlets inside of them. In other words, you can use flatbreads for almost anything you like. I remember how, as a child, I used to eat chapatti with a little butter and jaggery (an unprocessed sugar).

In almost every region of India, girls are traditionally taught the art of rolling chapattis at young age. In today's India, however, busy, working mothers are more likely to buy chapattis than prepare them at home, and they are sold fresh at almost all railroad, bus, and tram stations and some stores. In other countries, they are sold in Indian markets, where they can be found in packages on shelves and uncooked in the refrigerator sections.

Most Indian breads are either cooked on a flatiron skillet, pan fried, or deep-fried. In addition to chapattis, some of the most popular breads are puris, which are soft, puffed party breads that look like small balloons. Another popular variety is a triangular bread known as a "paratha," which is either layered or flat and has added spices and other ingredients.

Generally, a special round stand, either wooden or stainless steel, is used to roll Indian breads. These can be found in most Indian stores (although if you have a rolling board that you prefer, this will work just as well). The rolling pin that is used in most regions of India is very thin. These, called "belan," are also available in Indian stores. Some regions use a thicker rolling pin, though it is not quite as thick as the Western kind. A regular Western rolling pin may work, too.

Theplas are a spicy variety of parathas that are popular in India's western region, while naans – flat, leavened breads – are a specialty of Northern India. Theplas are typically eaten during travel. The dough generally does not need to rise or ferment.

Note: To knead or soften the dough when making these breads, I find that squeezing as much as I can hold in one hand and then moving it back and forth from one hand to the other, squeezing the dough until the dough is soft and without lumps, works well. If you are not used to make flatbread, it may require practice, especially in rolling and cooking them at the same time. Practice is important.

Recipes in This Chapter

Daily Roti

Making roti may seem like a long process, but once you know how to do it, you'll find it easy with some practice. Roti is considered to be a daily bread. It is very plain.

Recently, uncooked and ready rotis have become available in most Indian markets.

Rotis are generally cooked on each side on a skillet and then cooked directly over an open flame. If you do not want to cook on the flame, you can cook each side of the bread on the skillet and place them onto a plate, spreading ghee or butter on top to cover the surface. Rotis are meant to be served warm or fresh as they are being made. If this is not possible, cover them until ready to serve.

Utensils:

- Mixing bowls and covers
- Measuring cups
- A shallow bowl to hold flour for dipping the dough in before rolling it (I use one with a cover so that I can store the leftover flour for the next time I make roti)
- A rolling board
- A rolling pin
- A flat pan (lodhi) or a heavy metal skillet
- Spatulas, flat and slotted
- A plate to stack the roti on
- A clean tea towel to cover the roti and a small cloth to cover rolled rotis
- A bowl and a spoon for ghee or oil
- A knife
- A deep fryer shaped like a wok (for puris)

The following recipe is made with 2 cups of whole wheat flour and can be doubled.

Ingredients:

- 1½ cup whole wheat flour or multigrain flour
- 3 tablespoons white flour, kept aside for rolling the dough
- 1½ teaspoon vegetable oil
- ¼ teaspoon salt
- ½ cup warm water
- 1 tablespoon or less of ghee to spread on cooked roti (I use stick butter instead but substitute olive oil for butter to make recipe vegan)

The Process:

Put the whole wheat flour and salt into a bowl and add 1 teaspoon vegetable oil. Mix with the fingers of one hand.

Add the water. You may need less, depending on the brand of flour used. Using both hands, mix this until it forms into soft dough. Use the extra oil to knead the dough. Kneading by hand works best, since the dough is only about the size of a small ball.

Roll the dough into the shape of a log and cut it into eight equal portions. Roll each piece into balls. Put them back in the bowl and cover it.

Taking one ball at a time, flatten it with your hands and dip each side into the white flour. Put each ball onto the rolling board. Start rolling gently. You may need to dip the dough balls into the flour again if they stick to the board. Roll the balls until they are about 6 inches around. As a novice, you may need to roll all of the rotis before cooking any of them, keeping them separate and covering them with a clean kitchen towel.

In the meantime, heat the roti pan over medium heat. Sprinkle a drop of water onto the pan to make sure that it is hot. You are ready to start cooking roti.

Put one roti on the pan. It will start to bubble as it cooks, so turn it over to cook on the other side.
It will bubble again. Press it down slightly with the small cloth. There should be some brown spots on the roti at this point. Take the roti off of the pan and put it onto the plate, covering it lightly with butter or ghee.Finish making more rotis and stack them one on top of the other until done.

You are now ready to eat. Make sure to turn off the heat. To keep the rotis from drying, it is important to put them in a flat container with a lid. I often fold them twice into triangles so that they look nice and are easy to serve. There are some plastic containers available in the market for steaming. This type of container also works well for storing rotis.

Parathas

All parathas and theplas are made in similar way to the above recipe, just with a little more oil in the dough. They are then pan fried with very little oil. This recipe makes about 8 parathas and can be doubled.

Utensils:

- A bowl to make dough
- A rolling board
- A rolling pin
- A flat pan or skillet
- A small bowl for oil
- A spoon
- A spatula
- 2 plates
- A container for storing cooked parathas

Many varieties of parathas are listed below. They are all popular in Northern India. The process to make all but the laccha paratha is the same, but the ingredients of each type of paratha are different. It will be easy to make any variety of paratha once you know the typical process.

Spicy paratha with mung daal.

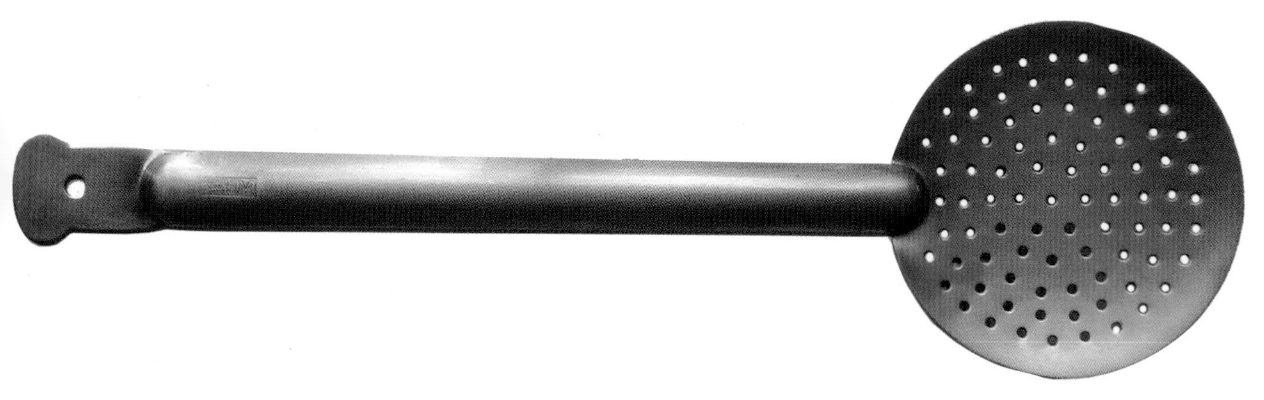

The Process of Making All Parathas

Dough:

Mix the dry ingredients and 2 tablespoons of oil. Add water and make the dough soft, but not sticky. Knead with both hands for about 3 to 5 minutes, using 1 teaspoon of oil.

Rolling:

Roll the dough into a log and cut it into eight or nine equal-sized pieces. Roll them into balls. Put them back into the bowl and keep them covered.

Take one ball out and dip it into the flour until it is coated. Press the ball gently down on the rolling board and start rolling. You may need to dip the partially rolled paratha into the flour again. Roll it until it is about 6 inches around. Put the rolled paratha on a plate and cover it with a cloth until all of the parathas are rolled. Make sure that they are not stacked, or they may stick to each other.

Cooking:

Heat the skillet on medium heat. When the skillet is hot (you can test this with a drop of water), put a paratha on it and use a small spoon to spread oil on the top surface. Use about ¼ teaspoon of oil. Make sure that the edges are oiled also.

The paratha will bubble slightly. Turn it over with a spatula and cover the other side with about ¼ teaspoon of oil.

When it bubbles some more, flip the paratha one more time. Make sure that the paratha has some light brown spots. Both sides of the paratha should be oiled.

Put the cooked paratha on a plate. It helps if the plate is lined with a paper towel to absorb oil. The cooked parathas can be stacked. Once all of the parathas are cooked and have cooled, cover them until you are ready to serve.

Parathas can be stored for 3 to 4 days in the refrigerator in a covered container or covered with foil.

Warm them on a skillet or in the oven before serving. Do not heat them in the microwave, as this makes them very tough.

Plain and Spicy Parathas

Plain Paratha 

Ingredients:

- 1½ cup whole wheat flour, chapatti flour, or multigrain flour
- 2 tablespoons oil + 1 teaspoon (to knead)
- ½ teaspoon salt
- ¼ teaspoon black pepper, ground
- ¼ teaspoon roasted cumin, crushed
- ½ cup or a little more of water
- 3 tablespoons vegetable oil to use in cooking the paratha*
- 3 tablespoons flour to use for rolling the dough

Spicy Paratha (Thepla)

Ingredients:

- 1½ cup of whole wheat, chapatti, or multigrain flour
- 2 tablespoons oil + 1 teaspoon (to knead)
- 3 tablespoons oil to use for cooking (You may not use all the oil)
- 3 tablespoons flour for rolling parathas*
- ½ teaspoon or more of salt (to taste)
- ½ teaspoon turmeric
- ½ teaspoon chili powder
- ½ teaspoon ginger-chili paste
- 2 tablespoons plain yogurt
- ⅓ cup or more warm water
- ½ teaspoon garlic paste (optional)

Methi Paratha

Add to above ingredients

- Add 1 tablespoon of fresh, chopped fenugreek leaves (methi) or kasuri methi and about ½ teaspoon of sugar while making the dough. You may need to use a little less water. Add a little water to the dough at a time. Knead, roll, and cook this paratha in the typical way.

Aloo Paratha 

Ingredients:

- 2 cups whole wheat flour, chapatti flour, or multigrain flour
- 1 medium-sized potato, boiled, peeled, and mashed
- ½ teaspoon ginger-chili paste
- 1 tablespoon chopped green onions
- 1 tablespoon chopped cilantro
- ½ teaspoon + a little more salt, to taste
- ½ teaspoon roasted cumin powder
- ½ teaspoon ground black pepper
- 2 tablespoons vegetable oil + 1 teaspoon to knead into the dough
- 3 tablespoons vegetable oil for cooking parathas*
- ¼ cup water (or as needed)

Rolling out the dough for spicy paratha.

Laccha Paratha 

This paratha is somewhat flaky, and its rolling process is a bit different. The filling needs to be added while the parathas are being rolled. The dough is made and cooked in the same manner, but rolling is different than the other parathas.

This process may seem long at first, but these parathas are very tasty. Once you learn how to make them, you may want to make them many times.
Make the dough using above the ingredients, knead it, and make three balls. The dough is slightly tougher. It may take a little time. Kneed is so the dough is together – the dough will be harder, almost like Playdough.

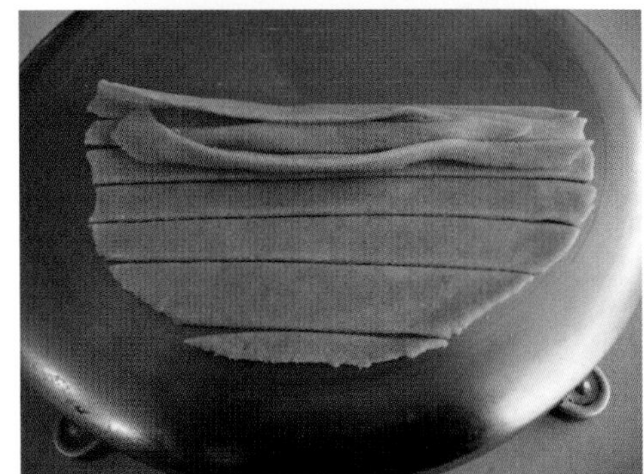

Ingredients for Dough:

- 2 cups whole wheat or chapatti flour
- 3 tablespoons oil + 1 teaspoon for kneading
- ½ teaspoon salt or to taste
- ½ cup warm water
- 4 tablespoons oil for cooking and spreading after rolled

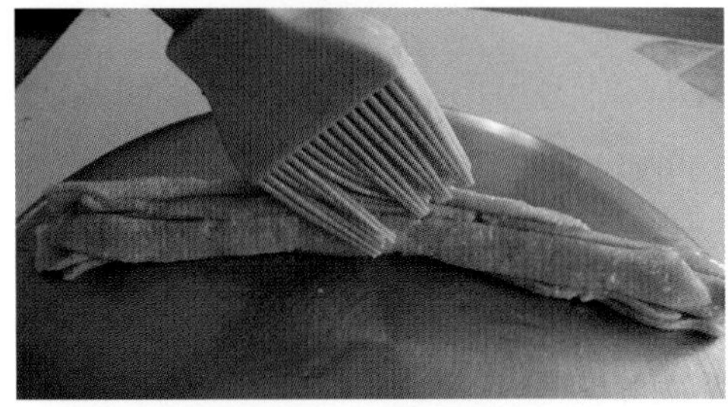

Ingredients for Filling:

- 1 teaspoon roasted ground cumin
- 1 teaspoon ground black pepper
- 1 teaspoon flour
- 1 tablespoon oil to spread with filling

The Process:

Mix the dry filling ingredients above in a bowl.

Make the dough using the above ingredients, knead it, and make three balls.

Using one of the three dough balls, roll a roti. Oil this roti on top and sprinkle a third of the filling from the bowl onto it, covering the flat area. Use your hands to roll the roti into a log and cut this into three pieces. Flatten each piece. Repeat this process with the other two dough balls. You will have nine balls to roll.

Roll each ball into a round paratha, making sure that the edges stay together. Now, use the pizza cutter and make very thin slices sideways as shown in the picture. Roll the slices in the same direction of the cut – see photo. Now gentle stretch this ling piece of sliced dough ad a little while stretching. Now make a wheel and make sure that the wheel does not separate. Press down the wheel a little and roll it in to a 6-inch round.

Pan-fry these parathas in the typical way.

Bhakri 

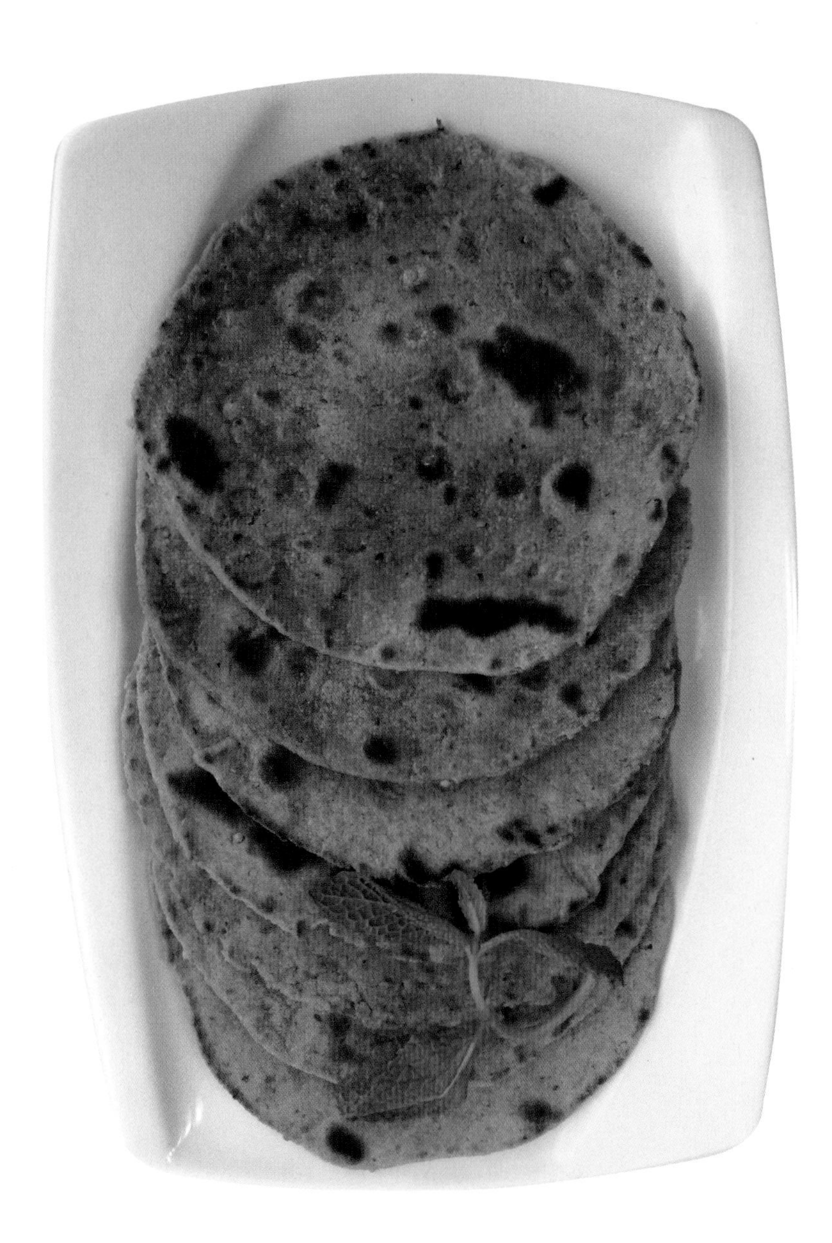

Bhakri is a dense and thick bread, mostly eaten at dinner time. Many families make this bread using ghee instead of oil. Generally, one vegetable or whole mung daals are served with this bread. Many families eat yogurt or jaggery with this bread. It is very easy to make.

The process of cooking it is slightly different than the process for paratha or roti. It has to be cooked at a low heat, and it will take a little longer. Makes about 6 bhakris.

Ingredients:

- 2 cups whole wheat flour or chapatti flour
- 4 tablespoons vegetable oil
- 1 teaspoon salt
- ¼ teaspoon sugar
- 1 tablespoon butter or ghee
- ½ teaspoon roasted cumin powder
- ¼ cup or less of water

Note: The dough will be harder than paratha dough and kneading is very important. When you roll bhakri, the edges may not be smooth, but it's okay. I found using covering rolling surface with parchment paper makes the rolling easier.

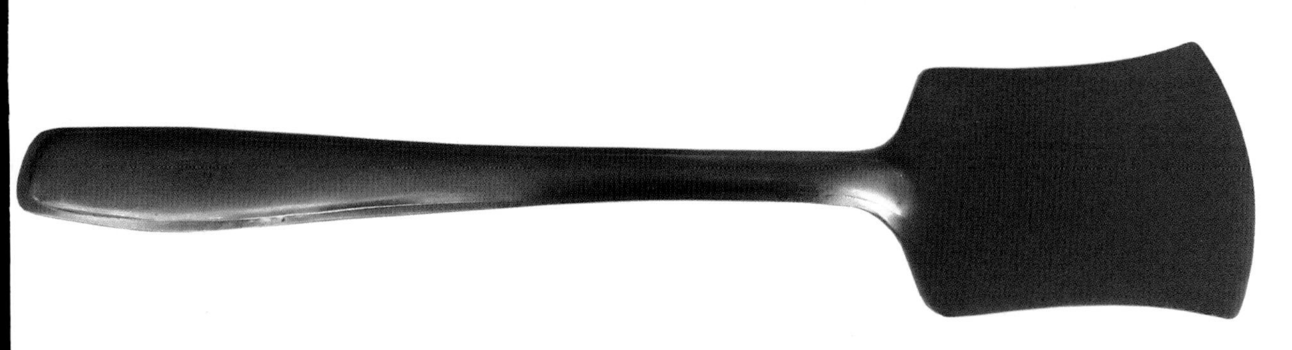

The Process:

Mix the dry ingredients, then add the oil. Once this is thoroughly stirred, add a little water at a time to make the dough. The dough should have the consistency of slightly hard but oily Playdough. Once the dough is formed, knead it using both hands. Make about eight equal-sized balls. Next, roll the bhakri into rounds that are 5 inches across and make some marks with a fork on top of each.

Heat the skillet at medium low heat. Once the skillet is hot, start cooking the bhakris. It will take a little while to cook these, since the heat is low. Let each cook for a minute or two. When you see brown spots on the bottom when checking with a spatula, flip the bhakri over. It is good to gently press the top side of it with a cloth and let it cook again. Once the brown spots appear on the second side, the bread will not have any uncooked surface. Put it on a plate and spread a little ghee over it. Repeat this process with all bhakris. Once they are done, you can stack them.

Serve the bhakris warm and enjoy. Leftover bhakris are also commonly served with chai tea the next morning. If you store them at room temperature in a container, they will be good for two to three days.

Puris 

Puris are fried "party breads" or breads that are made for special occasions. The consistency and kneading (softening) and rolling of the dough is very important in making Indian breads. Puris are rolled separately into small circles and flash fried. It may take a few tries for you to get them right, but don't be discouraged. These are a lot of fun to make, especially as a group with the participation of your family or friends. One person can knead the dough, another can roll it, and someone else can fry it. Frying is the most fun, since you get to watch the puris puff up like balloons in just seconds.

To knead or soften the dough, I find that squeezing it and then moving it back and forth from one hand to the other works well. The dough is then divided into equal-sized balls and rolled out into flat rounds. Before starting to roll, lightly oil the rolling surface. Do not use flour. If you find that the dough is too sticky, knead more flour into the dough prior to rolling. Oiling your hands before kneading will help keep the dough from sticking to your hands. The dough's consistency should be like smooth Playdough.

One heaped cup of whole wheat flour makes about 8 to 10 puris. Keep in mind that wheat flour varies from brand to brand, and some mixtures may need more water than others.

Chana and chole

Plain, Chole Puri, and Masala Puri 

This process might seem long, but keep in mind that it is easy to fry the puris once you've make the dough. Plain, chole, and masala puris are all made in the same way. The only differences are that chole puris are rolled to about 5 to 6 inches in size and are slightly thicker than other varieties, needing more dough, and masala puris have spices added to the dough. They are rolled to the same size as regular puris.

Utensils Needed:

- A mixing bowl
- A deep-frying pan, something like a small wok
- A slotted spoon to take puris from the frying pan
- A plate lined with paper towels to absorb oil
- A rolling pin and a rolling stand

Ingredients for Plain and Spicy Puris:

- 2 cups whole wheat flour
- 3 tablespoons oil for mixing into the dough + 1 teaspoon for kneading
- 2 to 3 cups oil for frying
- ½ teaspoon salt
- ¼ to ½ cup water

Note: To make spicy puris, add ½ teaspoon red chili powder, and ¼ teaspoon turmeric.

This recipe makes about 10 puris that are 3 to 4 inches in size. You can double the recipe to make more puris or bigger ones. You can also keep this recipe and make fewer puris of a larger size.

Chole Puri, or Bhatura

Some puris may not puff up, but this is normal.

Chole Puri (Bhatura) 

This Puri is generally made with white flour but in this recipe, whole wheat flour is used.

Ingredients:

- 2 cups whole wheat flour
- 1 cup enriched white flour
- 4 tablespoons vegetable oil + 1 teaspoon (for kneading)
- 2 cups vegetable oil for frying
- ½ teaspoon salt

The Process:

In the mixing bowl, mix the flour with the oil and salt to make dough. These are large in size and make about 10 to 12 puris. You do not need to sift the flour. Add about ¼ cup of water and mix it into the dough using your fingers. Use more water as needed to reach the right consistency. The idea is to roll the puris without using the flour, so the dough should have the consistency of playdough.

Use a portion of 1 teaspoon of oil to cover your

hands. Knead the dough using both of your hands until it has softened, about 3 to 5 minutes. Use the remainder of the teaspoon of oil in the kneading process as necessary.

Once the dough is workable, meaning that it can be rolled without breaking, roll it into a long rod and cut this into equal-sized sections. Roll these into balls with your hands. Press one ball at a time on the rolling board. Make sure that they do not stick to the surface. Use a bit of oil if needed.

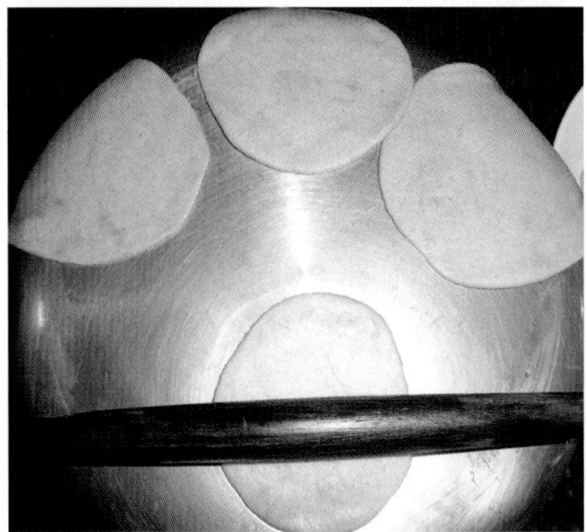

Note: It is a good practice to plan time for rolling and frying separately so that your full attention is given to each part of this process. Each part should only take a few minutes.

Start rolling the puris until they are about 3 inches in diameter. Put them on a plate, covering them with a paper towel so that they don't dry out. Dry puris may not puff.

Drop a tiny piece of dough into the oil to test it. It should come up floating right away.

Start frying one puri at a time. Each one should only take a few of seconds to puff up and float. Once it floats, turn it over for a few more seconds until it become a light golden color.

If a puri does not puff up, turn it over anyway after a few seconds. Some puris may not puff up, but this is normal.

Scoop each puri out of the oil and drain the extra oil for a couple of seconds by holding the slotted spatula on the side of the frying pan. Put the puris onto a paper towel-lined plate. Make sure not to put the fried puris on top of each other. This would make them deflate.

Serve fresh. Do not reheat puris in the oven. They do not need to be warm to taste delicious, and they may become hard and flat if rewarmed.

The Many Varieties of Roti—Indian Flatbreads

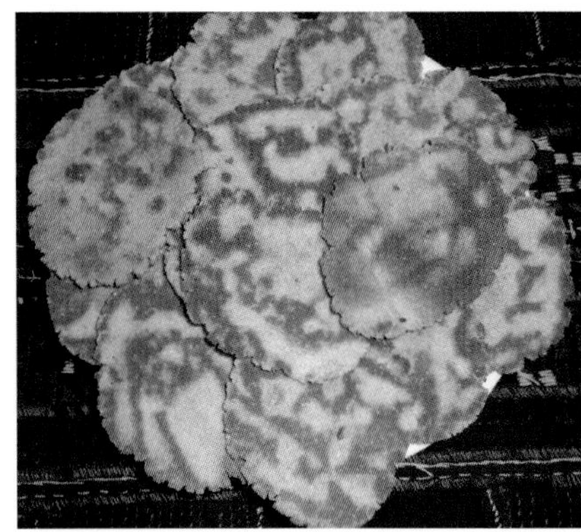

SWEET BHAKRI

METHI PARATHA

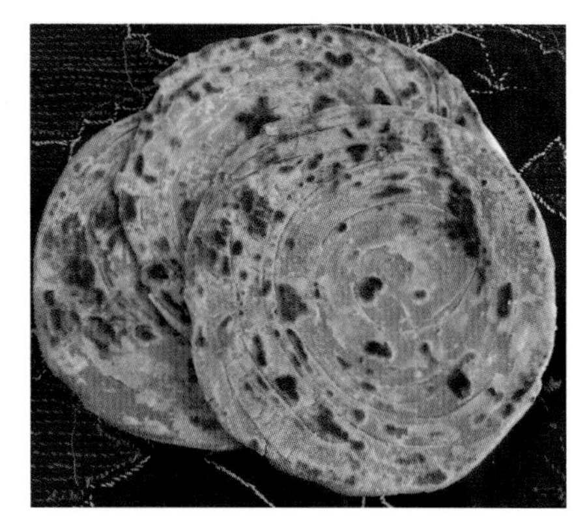

LACCHA PARATHA

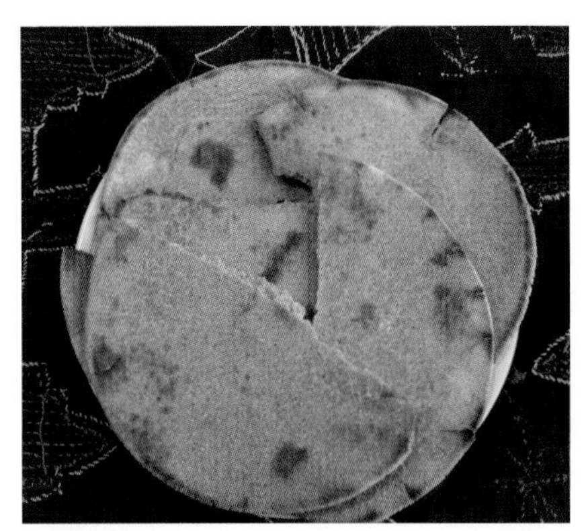

MILLET ROTI

MULTIGRAIN BHAKRI

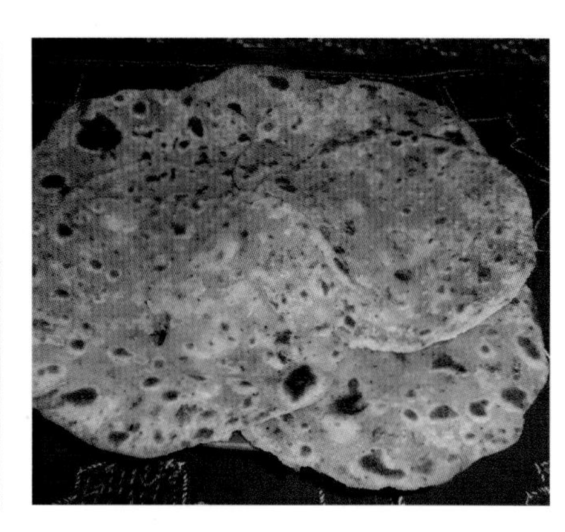

POTATO PARATHA

SPINACH PARATHA

DAILY ROTI FOLDED

SPICY PURI

Daals

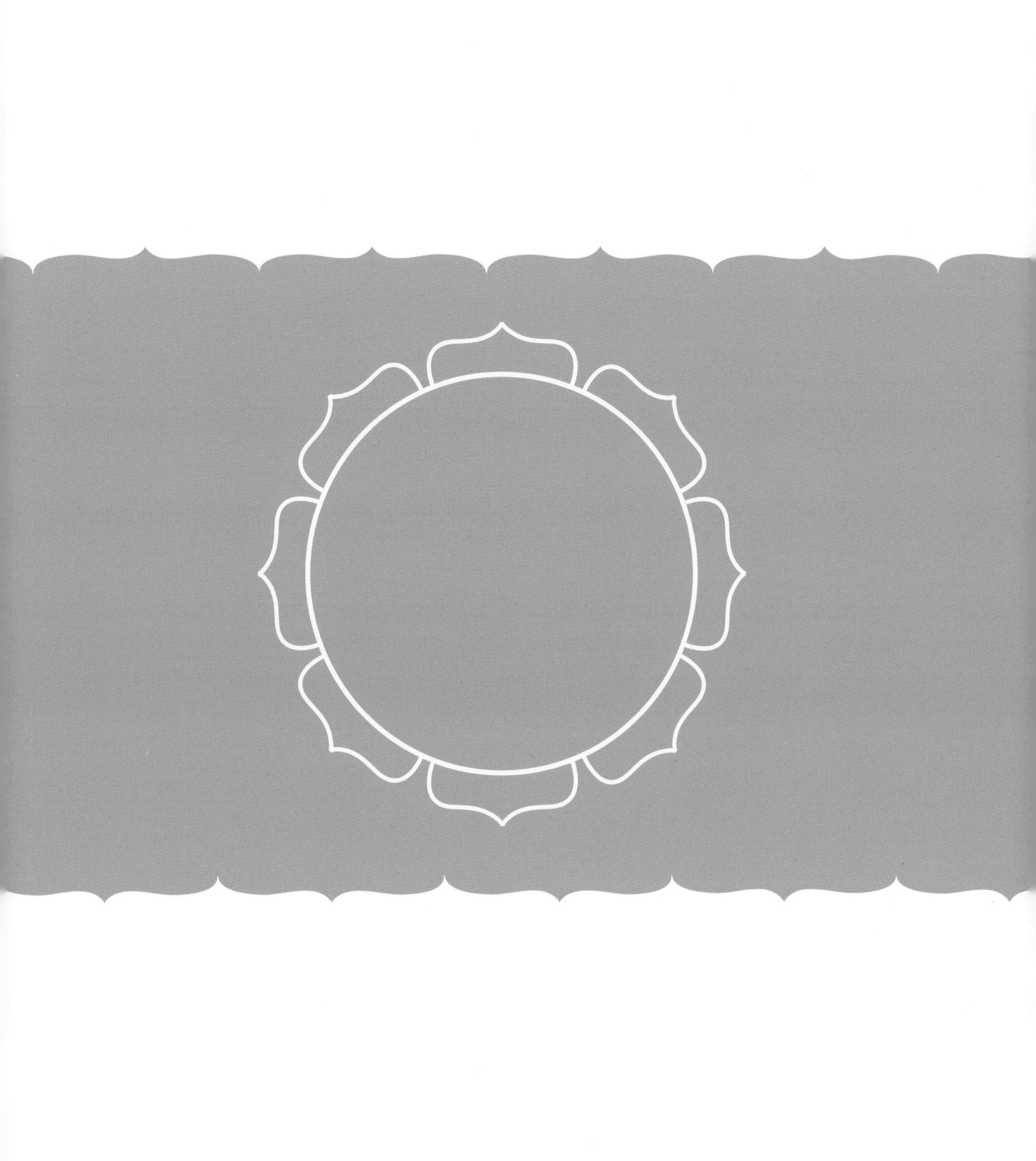

Daals

BEANS AND LENTILS

In Indian cuisine, "daal" refers to both the ingredient and the dish. Broadly speaking, it refers to legumes such as beans, peas, and most importantly, lentils. These legumes are hulled and sometimes split, then prepared into thick, hearty stews. Daals come in a variety of colors, shapes, and sizes. They make up a large part of the Indian meal as they are not only delicious, but healthy as well. Daals are also a huge source of protein in vegetarian diets and provide important dietary fiber. Daals make spicy and tasty soups, perfect for winter meals.

All uncooked or dry daals can be stored for months in a cool, dry place and will last for up to six months if properly stored. Almost all split daals are cooked via the same process, and all whole beans are prepared by the same process; the basic spices are typically the same. Once you learn the preparation process and know what spices to add, making daals will be easy.

Note: All daals, whether whole or split, must first be washed by hand in a bowl of warm water to get rid of sediments and then soaked for varying times, depending on what size and variety you are using. Split daals generally require 10 minutes to a half hour of soaking before cooking, except urad daal, which needs to be soaked for about 6 to 8 hours. Whole daals need more time, from 6 to 8 hours of soaking. When cooking daal in a pot, first boil water, then add the soaked daal beans. Daals are soaked for two reasons:
1—Soaking makes daals cook faster and leaves small impurities at the bottom. A sieve also works well to drain water and remove impurities. Daals double in quantity after being soaked and cooked.
2—There will be foam on top as the daal cooks. It is a good practice to scoop off the foam as it comes to the top.

The amount of water in the recipes are approximate amounts used. All daals are different, and some may absorb more water as they cook. Keep a watchful eye and add more water when needed. Making new and different types of food may take some practice. Whole beans and daals take longer time to cook may be from 20 minutes for whole mung to almost an hour for whole urad. Some daals and whole beans look similar after they are cooked, but they taste different.

Tadka

"Tadka" is an Indian word for "tempering." This process is used in preparing Indian food in which whole spices are roasted briefly in oil or ghee to enhance their flavors. Tadka is generally used at the beginning of cooking vegetables and curries, or as with daals, added at the end of cooking or just before serving.

Ingredients typically used in tadka include two or more of the following items: cumin seeds, black mustard seeds, fennel seeds, dried red chilies, fenugreek seeds, asafoetida, cloves, curry leaves, fresh green chilies, chopped onion, and garlic.

Hot oil is added to daals to help digest them.

A pressure cooker is a time saving utensil. The process is faster and boiling process will not be needed, and less water will be used. Follow the manufacturer's instructions and use it as directed. I use one that has a whistle. For whole beans, 3 whistles. This chapter also gives information on sprouting whole daals, and their uses.

English and Hindi names

English	Hindi
Black Gram	Urad whole / Kaali Daal
Black Eyed Peas	Chawli
Chickpeas	Chana Red
Garbanzo Beans	Kabuli Chana
Mung	Mung whole
Red Kidney Beans	Rajma
Red Lentil	Masoor whole
Split Chickpeas	Chana Daal
Split Black Gram	Urad Daal / Kaali Daal
Split Mung	Mung Daal
Split Lentil	Tuvar Daal / Arhar Daal
Split Red Lentil	Masoor Daal
Whole Lentil	Tuver Dana
Red Chowli	Azuko Beans

Utensils Needed for this Chapter:

- **A pot for cooking daal**
- **A bowl for washing and soaking daal**
- **A daal spoon or another large spoon for stirring**
- **A tadka pot**
- **A hand mixer (only needed for toor daal and kadhi)**
- **Measuring cups and spoons**
- **6 small bowls for ingredients**
- **A spice box**

Recipes in This Chapter

Mung Daal (V)

Of all daals, mung daal probably cooks the fastest and is the easiest to learn. It's the basic daal. It needs to soak for about 10 to 15 minutes. this daal cooks well without a pressure cooker. Mung daal can be made like a thick soup by using less water in the cooking process. 1½ cup of dry daal will make 4 to 6 servings, or about 4 to 5 cups.

Ingredients:

- 1½ cup mung daal
- 3 cups water for cooking daal
- About 2 to 3 cups warm water to soak daal
- ½ teaspoon salt or per taste
- 1 tablespoon ginger-chili paste or per taste
- ½ teaspoon garlic paste (optional)
- ¼ teaspoon turmeric
- 1 tablespoon chopped cilantro
- 1 tablespoon lemon juice

For Tadka:

- 1 tablespoon oil
- ¼ teaspoon each of cumin seeds, black mustard seeds, and chili powder (to add last)
- 3 to 4 curry leaves, *¼ teaspoon chili powder

The Process:

Hand wash the daal two to three times and soak it in warm water for 10 minutes. In the meantime, prepare all needed items.

When the water starts boiling, add the soaked and drained daal. As the daal boils, it will foam up at the top. Scoop the foam out if needed and reduce the heat to medium low.

As the daal cooks, add salt, turmeric, ginger-chili paste, and garlic. Stir occasionally and add water if needed. The daal will start to break up when cooked. Add lemon juice only after the daal is cooked.

Heat oil in the tadka pot for about ½ minute. Add cumin and mustard seeds. When they crackle, add curry leaves and chili powder and pour this mixture over the daal.

The daal is now ready to serve. You can keep it covered and reheat it at low heat before serving. Add cilantro for garnish.

Mung Daal with Palak 

This variation is a very popular northern Indian dish. You will see this in many restaurants.

Prepare mung daal as above, but add a cup of chopped spinach just before the daal starts to break — about 10 minutes into boiling. The frozen variety of spinach is okay, but fresh spinach is better. If you use frozen spinach, buy the pre-chopped kind and just defrost it before adding it to the daal.

Mung Daal with palak.

Mung Daal with Yogurt

Adding plain unsweetened yogurt to mung and urad daals gives them a tangy taste, and this is very popular in West Indian cuisine. To make these delicious daals, add about ½ cup of whisked yogurt to the daal just before adding the tadka and then boil it for about 2 minutes, stirring occasionally before serving.

Mung Daal with yogurt.

Of all daals, mung daal probably cooks the fastest and is the easiest to learn. It's the basic daal.

Urad Daal 

This daal needs soaking for about 6-8 hours. If you are going to make this daal in the evening, soak it in the morning. If you want to make it in the morning, soak it in the evening. Soak this daal after you wash it, making sure that the water runs clear of sediments. You will be using the water from the soaked daal in the cooking process as well. Urad daal takes a long time to cook — it may take as long as half an hour and may need more water, as the water will be continuously evaporating. This recipe works best in a pressure cooker. This daal is made especially for the village-style dinner. Urad daal, baingan bharta, and millet bread with garlic chutney is a special meal in the western state of Gujarat. Yields about 4 to 5 cups. Serves 4 to 6.

Ingredients:

- 1 ½ cup urad daal, washed thoroughly and drained
- 3 cups water for soaking + 2 to 3 cups to cook daal
- 1 teaspoon salt
- ½ teaspoon turmeric powder
- 1 teaspoon garlic paste
- 1½ teaspoon or more ginger-chili paste, per taste
- 1 teaspoon lemon juice (for serving)
- 1 teaspoon chopped cilantro

For Tadka:

- 1 tablespoon oil
- ¼ teaspoon black mustard seeds
- ¼ teaspoon cumin seeds
- 4 to 5 curry leaves
- ¼ teaspoon chili powder
- 1 1-inch stick cinnamon and 2 to 3 cloves (optional)

The Process:
Boil 2 cups of water at medium heat and add soaked daal. Add the remaining water in which the daal was soaked.

Bring this to a boil. Scoop off the foam and let the daal cook until it starts to break. Another way of checking the daal is to take two to three grains out with a spoon and press them with your finger. When cooked, they should break easily when you press. Add salt, turmeric, ginger-chili paste, and garlic. Once the daal is cooked, take it off the heat.

Heat oil in your tadka pot for about ½ minute. Add the cinnamon stick, cloves, cumin seeds, and black mustard seeds. They should start to crackle right away. Once the seeds crackle, take the oil off the heat and add the curry leaves and chili powder. They may splatter, so be watchful. Immediately pour this on top of the daal.

Heat the daal just before serving. Stir it, adding the cilantro and lemon juice.

Urad Daal with Yogurt

This daal is a very popular dish, especially with millet roti and baingan bharta. These three dishes are a specialty of Gujarat village food. Urad daal comes with and without shells. We have used urad daal without shells in regular urad daal, and daal with black shells in urad daal with yogurt – you can use the one you prefer. To make this daal, whisk ½ cup of yogurt and about 1 teaspoon of chickpea flour in a small bowl, make a paste, and add it to the the above daal recipe just before adding the tadka. Boil for about 2-3 minutes. This is a soupy daal.

Note: To make recipe vegan, remove yogurt from ingredient list.

Daal Makhani 

This daal is a specialty of northern India. Generally, this daal is cooked adding rajma (kidney beans). I use canned beans. Most northern Indians serve this daal. Black urad daal is the main ingredient in this recipe. This daal is whole urad daal with black shell. Soak this whole daal 4 to 6 hours The spices are different, and the process may seem time-consuming. Note: It is best to cook this daal in a pressure cooker so you can see the black shells floating. Scoop them out if possible. Yields about 4 to 5 cups. Serves 4 to 6. "Makhani" means "with butter," but this recipe is vegan.

Ingredients:

- 1 cup black urad daal, washed (soak for 8 hours)
- 3 cups water to soak + 2 to 3 cups of water to cook daal
- 1 onion, chopped (used for tadka)
- 2 medium-sized tomatoes, chopped (used for tadka)
- 1 teaspoon crushed garlic or garlic paste
- 2 tablespoons coriander-cumin powder
- 1 teaspoon ginger-chili paste
- 1 ½ teaspoon amchoor powder
- 1 teaspoon salt
- 3 pieces brown cardamom (If kept in daal for a longer period of time, this will become hot and spicy – remove before serving)
- 1 tablespoon chopped cilantro (for garnish)
- 1 teaspoon kasuri methi (Substitute with chopped fresh methi leaves, use kasoori methi, crushed)
- ½ cup cooked kidney beans (I used canned ones) Drain them. You will have leftover beans.) These beans are called RAJMA.

For Tadka:

- 1 tablespoon oil
- ½ teaspoon panch puran
- 1 onion, chopped

For Tadka (continued):

- 2 medium-sized tomatoes, chopped
- 1 teaspoon crushed garlic or garlic paste
- 2 teaspoons coriander-cumin powder

The Process:

For this daal, tadka is used first.

Heat oil in a pan – use this pan to make the daal. Add the panch puran, tomatoes, onions, and garlic. Sautée until the onions are soft and translucent and the tomatoes are like a paste. Add the coriander-cumin powder.

Add all the spices to the cooked daal. Make sure that there is enough liquid in the daal. Add the rest of the ingredients except the cilantro. Cook at low heat until the daal and spices are mixed, about 10 minutes.

Garnish with cilantro before serving.

Tuvar Daal / Arhar Daal 

This daal is made daily in the western part of India. Depending on the area, this daal can be very spicy. This daal is generally oiled and most Indian stores sell them rubbed with oil. This daal takes a longer time to cook, and need to soak for at least 2 to 3 hours. Use the pressure cooker, if you have it. Tuvar daal is generally fully cooked, and then the hand mixer is used to break it down to a paste. Water is added to give it the consistency of a thin soup. Spices are added, and then the mixture is boiled for a while so that the spices are totally mixed in and the aroma can be smelled in the home. Yields 4 to 5 cups. Serves 4 to 6.
Note: Hand mixer is needed for this recipe.

Ingredients:

- 1½ cup tuvar daal, washed and soaked in 2 cups of warm water for about 2 to 3 hours
- (For best results, use a pressure cooker – it also requires less water)
- 1 teaspoon salt or per taste
- 1 teaspoon jaggery powder
- 2 teaspoons coriander-cumin powder
- ¼ teaspoon turmeric powder
- ½ teaspoon chili powder
- 2 teaspoons ginger-chili paste or ½ chili cut in 1-inch long strips and 1-inch ginger, crushed
- 3 pieces kokum
- ½ teaspoon crushed garlic (optional)
- 1 medium-sized tomato, chopped
- 2 tablespoons chopped cilantro

For Garnish:

- 1 tablespoon chopped cilantro
- 1 teaspoon grated coconut

For Tadka:

- 1 teaspoon or a little more oil
- ¼ teaspoon black mustard seeds
- ½ teaspoon whole cumin seeds
- 4 to 5 curry leaves
- 4 cloves
- 1 small stick cinnamon
- 1 pinch asafetida (optional)
- 1 tablespoon raw shelled peanuts (optional)

The Process:

Wash the daal in warm water with your hands and soak it in two cups of warm water for 2 to 3 hours. Heat water to almost boiling, then add the soaked daal. Let the mixture come to a boil. Once it is boiling, turn down the heat so that the daal still boils, but does not boil over. Stir occasionally. This daal takes about ½ hour to cook. To check that the daal is cooked, take out a grain or two with a spoon and press them. The grains should press down to mush. Once cooked, turn off the heat and use the hand mixer to break down the daal into a smooth, liquid soup.

Put the daal on low medium heat again. Add salt, sugar, dry spices, ginger-chili paste, kokum, tomato, and garlic. Let the daal simmer. It is important to keep adding water if needed so that the daal does not sit at the bottom of the pan.

Heat oil in the tadka pot for about ½ to 1 minute. The oil must be hot to bring out the flavor in the seeds. Add the black mustard and cumin seeds, letting them crackle. Add the curry leaves and then add this whole mixture to the daal. It will sizzle and splatter, so be careful.

Let the daal simmer for another 5 minutes. You can cover it and keep it for 3 to 4 hours before serving. Serve it hot. It can be reheated. Make sure to add a little water when reheating, since the daal thickens.

Leftover daal can be kept in the refrigerator for up to 3 days and can be used for some South Indian dishes like Sambar or to make Daal Roti soup.

Kadhi

Kadhi is made differently in different regions. For example: In Punjab, it is served with chickpea flour fritters in it, while it has coconut milk added to it in Southern India. This is a dairy-based dish. Kadhi is made with yogurt and besan (chickpea / garbanzo bean flour). It is sometimes served instead of daal (lentils) in meals. Curry leaves are used for flavor and can be bought fresh in Indian stores. You can buy a bunch, dry it, and store the leaves in a jar. Kadhi can be made a day ahead of time, and it stays good for at least 3 to 4 days when refrigerated. This makes a wonderful yogurt soup in winter. It is always served hot. Kadhi should not be cooked in a pressure cooker. Yields about 5 cups. Serves 4 to 6.

Note: To make recipe vegan, replace yogurt with coconut milk.

Plain Kadhi

This is a wonderful yogurt soup that goes well with rice, pilaf, and khichari.

Ingredients:

- 1 and ½ cup plain yogurt (Low-fat yogurt is fine)
- 3 to 4 cups water
- 3 tablespoons besan flour
- 1 teaspoon salt
- 1 tablespoons jaggery powder
- 1 whole green chili, cut in half lengthwise and then cut in half to make 4 pieces
- 2-inch piece of fresh ginger, finely chopped or crushed
- 1 tablespoon chopped cilantro (half to add while cooking, and half to use as a garnish)
- ¼ teaspoon methi seeds

For Tadka:

- About 6 curry leaves, fresh or dried
- ½ teaspoon cumin seeds
- ½ teaspoon black mustard seeds
- 4 cloves
- 1-inch stick of cinnamon
- 1 dried red chili (if you'd like it to be spicy)

The Process:
In a large pot, mix the chickpea flour / besan with ½ cup of water until it is a smooth paste. Add the yogurt and use the hand mixer to mix the yogurt and besan paste together. This may foam a little at the top, which is okay. Mixing it with a spoon will form lumps.

Add the remaining water, salt, jaggery, green chili, ginger, and methi seeds and stir well. Cook at medium heat, stirring often (though not continuously) so that it doesn't curdle or separate. Bring to a boil and turn the heat down and let it simmer for about 5 minutes. You can take the pot off the heat and keep for a couple of hours.

Heat oil in a tadka pan. Wait for about ½ a minute, add the cumin and black mustard seeds, cloves and, cinnamon stick. When the seeds begin to pop and the spices become fragrant, remove from heat, add dried red chili (if you want it spicy). Add curry leaves, and pour the mixture over the kadhi.

Heat the kadhi just before serving and garnish it with cilantro.

Variation 1: Vegetable Kadhi

Add ½ cup total of chopped vegetables like onions, green beans, and tomatoes when cooking this recipe.

Variation 2: Mango Kadhi

This is a very popular dish in western India called "fajeto." It is mainly prepared during the mangoes season when varieties of ripe and sweet mangos are available. Now with the refrigeration and availability of canned mango juice, this dish is prepared any time. Extra ingredients needed: ½ cup canned mango pulp, cut into cubes; and 1 mango with the skin removed.

To make fajeto, use the above plain kadhi recipe but omit jaggery and use ½ cup of fresh or canned mango pulp / purée added to the yogurt and chickpea flour. Use the same process as kadhi. The color of fajeto is slightly yellow due to the color of mango pulp. Add fresh mango pieces cut into small cubes just before serving. Garnish with cilantro.

Vegan kadhi.

Mango kadhi.

Whole Mung, Urad, and Lentil 

Cooking whole daals in a pressure cooker will save a lot of time. All whole bean daals are cooked in the same way, but the spices and other ingredients may vary. All whole daals need soaking for about 8 hours. You can soak only mung for less time – aboutt 2 to 3 hours. Whole bean daals will double in size and quantity after soaking, and most of the water will be absorbed, so you may need to add more. You can add or reduce the spices to your taste.

Note: When you boil whole daal beans, the skin of the beans will float to the top. You can scoop this out, if possible. It's okay to leave some of the skin. It is not harmful. Turn off the heat once they are broken. Stir them gently to mix. This dish has consistency of thick soup. Yields about 5 cups. Serves 4 to 6. This recipe can be used for whole mung and urad.

Ingredients:

- 1 ½ cup whole daal beans, washed
- 3 cups water to soak
- 2 to 3 cups water to cook whole daal
- 1 teaspoon ginger-chili paste or 1 green chili and a 1-inch piece of ginger, peeled and chopped
- 1 teaspoon salt
- 2 teaspoons coriander-cumin powder
- ¼ teaspoon or a little more turmeric
- ½ teaspoon chili powder
- 1 to 2 tablespoons lemon juice (or to taste, for serving) depending on your taste
- ½ teaspoon sugar
- ½ teaspoon garlic paste

For Garnish:

- 1 tablespoon chopped cilantro
- 1 teaspoon grated coconut

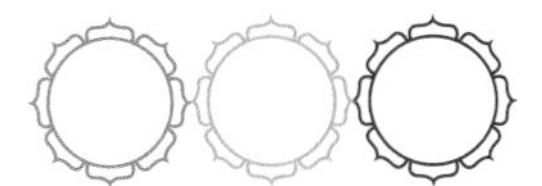

For Tadka:

- 1 tablespoon oil
- ½ teaspoon cumin seeds
- ½ teaspoon black mustard seeds
- 4 curry leaves
- 4 cloves, a 1-inch stick of cinnamon

The Process:

Heat about 2 cups of water. Rinse the soaked mung and add them to the hot water in the pot.

Add the salt and all of the spices. Add the ginger-chili paste and garlic after about 5 minutes. Let the beans cook for about 10 to 15 minutes – whole urad will take about 30 to 40 minutes. Add more water if needed to make sure that there is always water in the pot and mung beans do not stick at the bottom. Sometimes, beans may take longer to cook. The way to check that they are cooked is to take two or three beans out with a spoon and press them. They should be soft and mushy when pressed. Take the pot off the heat.

Heat the oil in the tadka pot for about half a minute. Keep watchful eyes: do not let the oil get too hot. Add the tadka spices. They will crackle, so be careful. Add the curry leaves and pour the tadka mixture over the cooked mung right away. Cooked mung beans can he reheated, and any leftovers can be saved in the refrigerator for a couple of days.

Add lemon juice before serving and garnish with cilantro and coconut.

Mung beans can be served with rice, roti, or any bread.

Alternative: To make Khatta Mung or mung with yogurt, mix ½ cup yogurt, 1 tablespoon besan / chickpea flour, and ½ cup water into smooth paste. Cover, heat, and serve as above.

Whole Urad Daal 

Whole urad daal takes longer to cook, so it would be time saving to use a pressure cooker in this case. The process and the spices are the same as with whole mung beans. You may need to use more water and a longer cooking time. Whole urad daal can also be made with yogurt and the same ingredients as khatta mung in order to make khatta daal. However, adding yogurt will make this recipe non-vegan.

Photo of daal shown here is not vegan.

Whole Lentil Daal 

Lentils are like whole tuvar daal which may take longer to cook depending on the variety. This recipe is like a spicy lentil soup.

Whole lentils will need to be soaked for about 2 hours. This dish is very easy to make. Lentils are available in bulk and in packets in most supermarkets. This dish can be served with rice or any roti of your choice. Yields 5 to 6 cups. Serves 4 to 6.

Ingredients:

- 1 and a ½ cups lentils
- 3 to 4 cups of water to soak lentils + 1 to 2 cups to cook lentils
- 2 tablespoons tamarind pulp
- ½ teaspoon salt or to taste
- ¼ teaspoon turmeric powder
- 2 teaspoons coriander-cumin powder.
- 1 teaspoon ginger-chili paste
- ½ teaspoon sugar (any kind you prefer)
- 1 tomato, chopped
- 1 tablespoon chopped cilantro + some for garnish
- 1 teaspoon lemon juice
- 1 small onion, chopped

Note: Any leftover chutneys can be used in any daal to enhance the taste

For Tadka:

- 1 tablespoon oil
- ½ purple onion, chopped
- ¼ teaspoon each black mustard and cumin seeds
- 3 to 4 curry leaves
- ½ teaspoon red chili powder-use it just before pouring over lentil

The Process:

Wash and soak lentils for up to 2 hours.

Boil about 2 cups of water and add drained lentils. Let the lentils boil for about 5 to 10 minutes at low heat, remove the foam from the top, and add water if needed. (*Note:* continued on next page)

After the lentils start to break, add salt, and dry spices and ginger-chili paste and chopped tomato. Let the spices blend in and cook for about 5 more minutes.

For Tadka: Heat oil in a tadka pot over low-medium heat for about ½ minute; add onions and let them cook for about one minute or slightly more.

Add dry seeds and curry leaves once the seeds start to sizzle and crackle. Add chili powder and pour the oil over the lentils. Stir and add lemon juice and chopped cilantro.

To serve: Garnish with cilantro and chopped onion and serve hot.

Whole Chana Amti

Chanas are red chickpeas that are available in Indian markets. Amti is a slightly tangy soup / daal. The process of washing and soaking this daal is the same as with any other whole daal, but the ingredients are slightly different. This is a popular whole daal. Yields about 5 cups. Serves 4 to 6.

Ingredients:

- 2 to 3 cups whole chana, washed and soaked overnight
- 2 to 3 cups water to cook with (you may need a little more water)
- ½ medium-sized onion, finely chopped
- 1 small tomato, finely chopped
- 1 teaspoon salt
- 2 tablespoons coriander-cumin powder
- 1 teaspoon ginger-chili paste
- ½ teaspoon garlic paste
- ½ teaspoon sugar
- ¼ teaspoon or a little more turmeric
- ½ teaspoon chili powder (or to taste)
- 1 tablespoon tamrind pulp (only added after the chana is cooked)

For Garnish:

- 2 tablespoons chopped cilantro

Enhancer:

- ½ cup each of yogurt and water, water – add 2 teaspoons chana flour with the amchoor for taste

The Process:

This is the same process as with the other whole beans.

Chana takes a long time to cook — at least half an hour. A pressure cooker may work best. Please note that chana that is cooked in a pressure cooker or covered will change its color to a dark brown. To find out if the chana is cooked, take a few beans in a spoon and press them.

After the chana is cooked and all of the spices are added, add the tamarind pulp and boil the mixture for about 5 minutes. This soup should not be very watery.

How to Sprout Whole Beans

Note: All these beans are available in Indian Market. Muth beans are like small and brownish mung beans. A visit to an Indian market may be helpful.

Indian cuisine uses sprouted mung beans, urad beans, chana, and lentils. The process of sprouting these may seem a little time-consuming, but these sprouted beans not only taste great: they have unlimited uses once you start getting creative.

Once soaked and sprouted, these beans will double and sometimes triple in volume. One cup of mung beans will make about 2 to 3 cups of sprouted beans. Soaking the beans in warm water is essential. Sprouting is the same process for all beans, and they take the same time to sprout, except that chana / chickpeas may take a little longer. I soak the beans in the morning and sprout them at night. By the next morning, the beans are sprouted. The process takes about 16 to 20 hours. These sprouts are different from the ones that you buy in the market. The sprouts will be small, and the beans will have a nutty taste.

Sprouted beans can be used as a topping on salads or just be cooked like whole beans with less water. They taste nutty and different.

Utensils needed:

- Bowls to wash and soak the beans and to sprout them in
- A strainer / colander
- A measuring cup
- A paper towel or cloth to cover the beans

Ingredients:

- 1 cup whole mung beans, urad beans, or chana

The Process:

Wash the beans in a bowl with tap water, squeezing and rubbing them between your hands. Rinse them and repeat this process at least twice. Drain the beans in a colander, then put them back into the bowl and add 3 cups of warm water.

Cover and keep for 8 hours. The size will almost double. Drain the beans again and put them back into the bowl. Gently press a cloth or paper towel on top of the beans. Make sure the cloth or paper towel touches the beans when you cover them.

Leave this covered bowl in a warm place for 8 to 10 hours. I use the oven and keep the oven light on. You will then see the sprouted beans within 8 to 10 hours. You can freeze them, cook them, or use them raw. Just make sure to soak them in water for a few minutes before eating raw.

Sprouted Whole Mung Daal 

All sprouted and whole daal beans are cooked in similar way with similar spices. Cooking time may vary. Yields about 5 to 6 cups. Serves 4 to 6.

Ingredients:

- 2 to 3 cups sprouted mung (1 cup makes about 2 to 3 cups after sprouting)
- 2 cups water to cook sprouted beans (may need more for other beans)
- 1 teaspoon ginger-chili paste or ½ chili and a 1-inch long piece of ginger peeled and chopped
- 1 teaspoon salt
- 2 teaspoons coriander-cumin powder
- ¼ teaspoon or a little more turmeric
- ½ teaspoon chili powder
- 1 to 2 tablespoons lemon lemon juice (or to taste, for serving)
- ½ teaspoon sugar
- ½ teaspoon garlic paste

For Garnish:

- 1 tablespoon chopped cilantro
- 1 teaspoon chopped onion

For Tadka:

- 1 tablespoon oil
- ½ teaspoon each cumin seeds and black mustard seeds
- 4 cloves (optional)
- 1-inch stick of cinnamon (optional)
- 4 curry leaves (optional)

The Process:

Heat about 2 cups of water. Rinse the sprouted mung and add them to the hot water in the pot.

Add the salt and all of the spices. Add the ginger-chili paste and garlic after about 5 minutes. Let the Mung cook for about 10 to 15 minutes. Add more water if needed to make sure that there is always about 1 cup of water in the pot. Sometimes, mung beans may take longer to cook. The way to check that they are cooked is to take two or three beans out with a spoon and press them. They should be soft and mushy when pressed. Take the pot off the heat.

Heat the oil in the tadka pot for about a minute. Keep watchful eyes: do not let the oil get too hot. Add the tadka spices. They will crackle, so be careful. Add the curry leaves and pour the tadka mixture over the cooked mung right away. Cooked mung beans can he reheated, and any leftovers can be saved in the refrigerator for a couple of days.

Add lemon juice before serving and garnish with cilantro and coconut.

Mung beans can be served with rice, roti / paratha, and kachumber.

Alternative: To make sprouted mung with yogurt, mix ½ cup yogurt, 1 tablespoon besan / chickpea flour, and ½ cup water into smooth paste. Add to the mung before adding tadka. Cover and heat at a low temp; garnish and serve.

Note: Sprouted chana and red choli beans are made the same way. Chana will take a few minutes more to cook.

If you prefer less watery-soupy, make sure it is cooked well and cook till almost all water is evaporated. Take it off the heat.

Mixed Whole Beans Misal

This dish is not only a daal, but is served with rice or paratha and kachumber to make a complete meal. Misal is a dish from the state of Maharashtra in Southwest India. The actual dish is different, but I wanted to give it a unique appeal and aroma. If you intend to make this dish, you will need to plan ahead as all beans need to be soaked. This dish can be made with sprouted beans as well.

Making this dish might seem like a long process, as a few different types of whole beans will need to be soaked. There are also many other ingredients. This makes a great buffet party dish with rice or paratha and kachumber. Since this dish is served with many toppings, it can be very tasty and special meal. It is full of protein and other nutrients. This is a time-consuming dish to prepare and has 3 to 4 steps. You will need 4 soaking bowls. The whole beans may triple in size once soaked. This recipe requires sev-Indian thin noodles made from chic pea flour. Tamarind and date chutney can be purchased in Indian market. Fried noodles can be substituted for sev. Yields about 10 cups. Serves 8 or more.

Ingredients:

- 1 cup each whole mung, red chowli, whole chana, red whole muth beans and 2 medium-sized onions, chopped (1 for the tadka and half for the topping; If available, I use fried onions instead of fresh ones for the garnish)
- 2 medium-sized potatoes, peeled and cubed
- 3 to 4 cups of water, or 1 cup in the pressure cooker and 2 cups to add to beans while cooking
- ½ cup frozen mixed vegetables (peas, corn, green beans, carrots)
- 1½ teaspoon salt
- 1 teaspoon garlic paste
- 3 tablespoons coriander-cumin powder
- ½ teaspoon turmeric
- 2 teaspoons or more ginger-chili paste
- 3 teaspoons amchoor powder or 1 teaspoon tamarind paste

For Tadka:

- 2 tablespoons oil
- ½ teaspoon each of whole black mustard, cumin, fenugreek, kalonji, and fennel seeds
- ½ onion from above, chopped
- 4 to 5 curry leaves

For Garnish:

- 1 cup date chutney
- 1 cup plain yogurt, whisked to smooth (Omit yogurt to make vegan)
- ½ cup cilantro, chopped
- ½ onion, chopped (or fried onions if available in the market)
- 1 cup small sev, available in Indian markets (substitute with thin fried noodles if sev not available)

The Process:

Wash and soak the mung, chana, and muth beans separately for about 8 hours.

This may take about an hour to cook. Use medium high heat. A pressure cooker will save cooking time. Boil 2 to 3 cups of water. Add the chana and muth first, cook for about 20 to 30 minutes. Make sure that the foam is scooped out and that there is enough water.

Add the mung beans and chowli and cook for about 20 more minutes add potato cubes and mixed vegetables. Cook for another 10-15 minutes. You can use this time to cook the rice or make paratha, cut the onions, chop the cilantro, and whisk the yogurt. Yogurt should be a batter consistency and may need more water.

Once the beans are cooked (you can check this by pressing a few beans and seeing if they are mushy), add the mixed vegetables and cook until all are well-mixed and soft. This dish is a soupy dish and should have enough water-sauce.

Add the salt and all other spices and cook for 10 minutes at low heat. Stir occassionally

The Tadka:

Heat oil in a pan, add ½ of chopped onion and sautée it until it is a light brown.
Add all of the seeds and let them crackle. Add the curry leaves, then add the tadka mixture to the cooked misal.

To Set the Table and Serve:

Set out plates and soup bowls or large daal bowls as well as spoons and napkins.

Prepare bowls of chopped cilantro, onions, fried onions, yogurt, date chutney, and / or sev noodles.

Put the misal in the bowl. Top it with the yogurt. Add the date chutney, onions, and cilantro, topped with the sev. Serve with kachumber and paratha.

Red Chowli

Rice and Pilafs

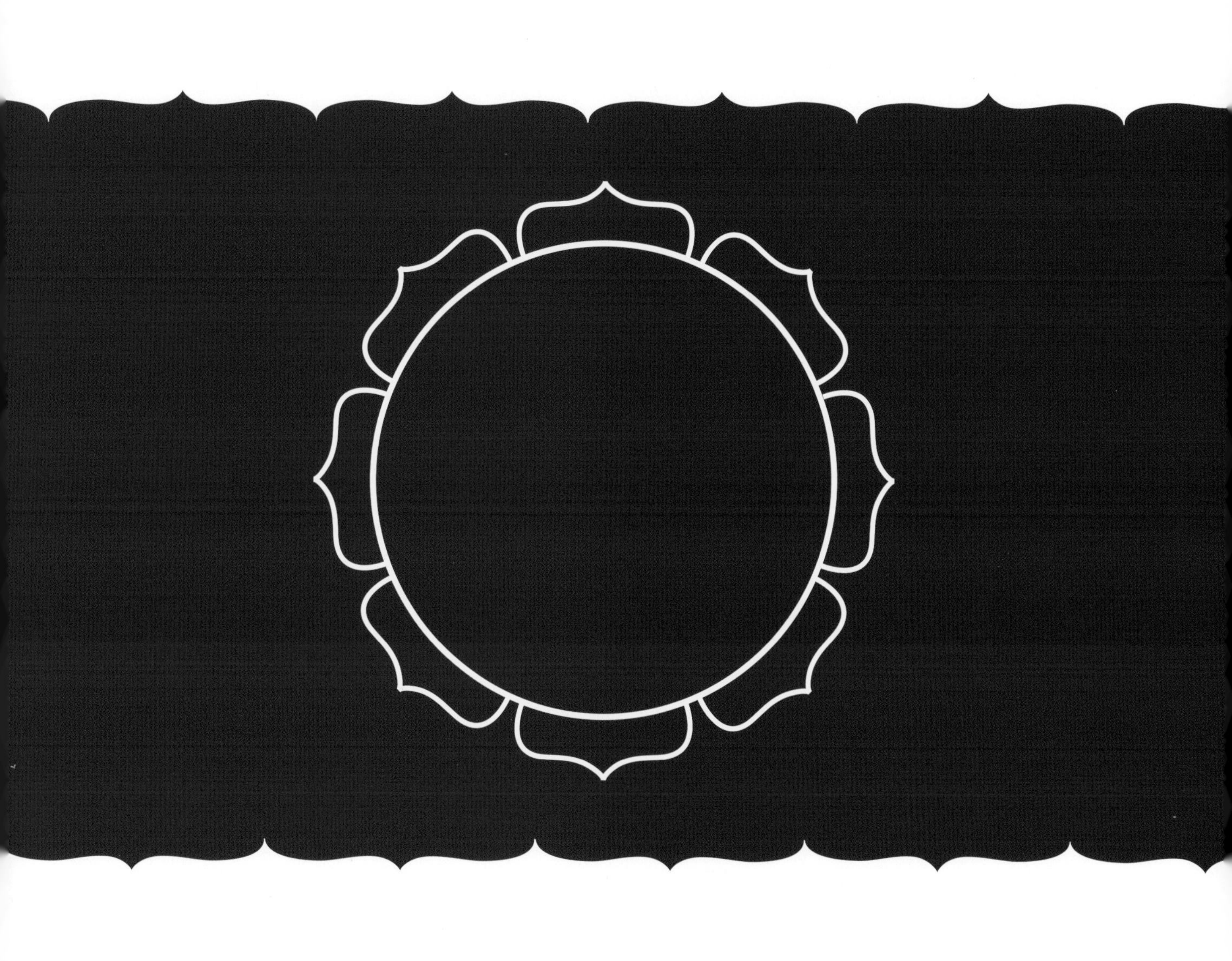

Rice and Pilafs

Rice is a main dietary staple of the Indian household. The most popular kind of rice is basmati, which can be bought in supermarkets and Indian grocery stores. In India, however, basmati is considered a rich person's rice. It is normally aged for at least three years. It is best to rinse the rice in cold water while squishing it with one hand. Drain it, and soak it for a few minutes, which makes it cook faster.

Many varieties of rice are available. Some kinds are used for particular recipes, and replacing those with basmati might not give you the same results. Indian recipes generally use long-grained or basmati rice; pearl rice is used in some sweet dishes. Red rice is a popular rice in South India.

Rice is also used to make some sweet dishes, such as kheer (rice pudding with no eggs), sweet coconut rice, and sweet rice with brown sugar. Dishes like dahi rice, lemon rice, jeera rice, sweet rice, and kheer can also be made from leftover rice.

Rice noodles, vermicelli, poha (flat rice), couscous, and quinoa can be used instead of rice and are cooked in the same way. This lets you create a variety of dishes, and some of them can be made ahead of time like rice or used to make pilaf or biryani. As with pasta, you can drain the rice when it is almost cooked, rinse it under tap water while it is still in the strainer, and put it back into the pot.

Cooking Rice:

This chart shows the approximate amount of water and cooking time needed to cook 1 cup of rice (dry-measured) on the stovetop. For better results, soak the rice for 10 to 20 minutes after measuring it.

For 1 cup of rice soaked-low to medium heat		
Type of Rice	**Amount of Water**	**Time Cook**
Short- or medium-grained rice	1 ½ to 2 cups of water	7 to 10 minutes
Long-grained rice	2 to 3 cups of water	10 to 15 minutes
Basmati rice	2 to 3 cups of water	7 to 10 minutes
Brown rice	3 cups of water	20 + minutes
Wild rice	3½ cups of water	20 + minutes

Pilaf is a dish that originally came from Persia. It is usually made with rice and vegetables or legumes, as well as a mix of spices.

Biryani was introduced to India by the Moguls, who ruled in the 1500s. It is a kind of pilaf with many extra items and spices.

For vegetarian pilaf, plain water and aromatic spices can be used to cook vegetables and rice together. Generally, dried fruits and fried nuts are added with a tadka. In pulao, the meat and rice are stirred before cooking. In biryani, they are clustered (layered) during the cooking process.

Utensils Needed for this Chapter:

- A bowl to soak the rice
- A pot to cook it
- A tadka pot
- A spoon
- A spatula and stirring spoons
- A chopping board and a knife
- Measuring cups and spoons
- A colander to strain rice
- A nonstick skillet or pan
- Some small bowls

Recipes in This Chapter

Plain Rice 

These recipes are meant to serve 4 to 6 people and call for 1½ cups of rice. This can easily be doubled – just check the cooking time. Freshly cooked rice adds a great flavor to any meal. Yields 3 cups. Serves 4 to 6.

Ingredients:

- 1 ½ cups basmati rice
- 2 to 3 cups water (for soaking)
- 3 cups water (for cooking, add as needed)
- ½ teaspoon salt
- 1 teaspoon oil

The Process:
Wash the rice and soak it for 10 minutes.

Bring 3 cups of water to a boil in the pot. Add the soaked, drained rice and turn the heat down to medium-low. Stir once, add the salt, and half-cover the pot with a lid. Let cook 7 to 10 minutes, stirring once or twice. To check that the rice is cooked, take out a grain or two with a small spoon and press gently. The grains should flatten into mush or be slightly firm. They should not be sticky or over-cooked. Cover the pot and let the rice steam once it is cooked.

If you want to strain the rice, take it off of the heat, pour it into the colander, run cold water over it, and return it to the cooking pot.

Add salt and oil. Gently turn the rice with a fork. Cover it.

Dahi (Yogurt) Rice

Dahi rice is easily made from leftover rice. It's great to eat with a meal or by itself. This dish is often made when people travel on trains or far from home because it stays good through the heat of the day. The probiotic nature of the yogurt also helps during travel. Yields 4 cups. Serves 4 to 6.

It's important not to heat the yogurt directly, as it will release water, which is undesirable.

Ingredients:

- 3 to 4 cups cooked rice
- 1 teaspoon salt
- 1 cup plain yogurt, whisked to remove lumps
- ½ teaspoon ginger-chili paste
- ½ teaspoon chopped cilantro, for garnish
- ¼ teaspoon turmeric powder (optional)

For Tadka:

- 1 tablespoon oil
- 1 cup chopped onions
- ½ teaspoon urad daal or dalia (optional)
- ½ teaspoon cumin seeds
- ½ teaspoon black mustard seeds
- 1 star anise
- 3 to 4 cloves, whole
- 4 to 5 curry leaves
- 1 1-inch cinnamon stick

The Process:

Make the rice as above, or use 3 to 4 cups of leftover rice. (If you use leftover rice, it's best to warm it in the microwave first.)

In a bowl, whisk yogurt and add salt, turmeric, and ginger-chili paste. Mix gently with a spoon.

Heat the oil in a pot (large enough to hold rice and yogurt mixture) for about 1 minute, keeping watchful eye on it. Add the urad daal or dalia and the chopped onion, cumin seeds, mustard seeds, star anise, and cloves, and let it cook for about 2 minutes. Finally, add the curry leaves.

Add the rice in to the pot. Stir gently so that the rice does not break up. Add the yogurt mixture, gently mix again, and remove from the heat. Garnish with chopped cilantro and serve.

Lemon Rice 

This can be made from either fresh or leftover rice. Yields 3 cups. Serves 4 to 6.

Ingredients:

- 3 cups cooked rice
- 1 teaspoon salt, or to taste
- 1/8 teaspoon (or a pinch) turmeric powder
- 2 tablespoons lemon juice
- 1 teaspoon cilantro, for garnish

For Tadka:

- 1 tablespoon oil
- 1/2 teaspoon cumin seeds
- 1/2 teaspoon black mustard seeds
- 4 cloves
- 1 1-inch cinnamon stick
- 4 curry leaves

The Process:

Warm the leftover rice or make freshly cooked rice.

Add the salt and turmeric powder.

Heat the oil in a nonstick pot for 1 minute or less, watching carefully. Add the cumin and black mustard seeds and let them crackle for a few seconds. Add the cloves, cinnamon, and curry leaves. Add the rice mixture and stir gently stir with a wooden spoon until the oil has coated the rice.

Add the lemon juice and mix again.

Top with cilantro and serve warm.

Pilaf for Maharani 

Yields 5 to 6 cups. Serves 6 to 8.

Ingredients:

- 1½ cups basmati rice, washed and soaked in 2 cups of water
- 3 cups water (for cooking)
- 2 tablespoon oil
- ½ cup chopped red onion
- 1 cup mixed vegetables, diced (green beans, peas, corn, and carrots)
- ½ teaspoon salt
- ¼ teaspoon sugar
- 1 tablespoon cilantro, chopped, for garnish

For Tadka:

- 1 tablespoon oil
- ½ teaspoon cumin seeds
- ¼ teaspoon black mustard seeds
- 4 cloves
- 2 star anise
- 4 curry leaves
- 4 cup raw shelled peanuts (optional)
- ¼ cup raw cashews chopped
- 2 tablespoon dried cranberries
- ½ cup golden raisins

The Process:

Start cooking the rice in a pot. Don't overcook it — slightly undercooked is better, because it will be reheated. The normal cooking ratio is 1 cup of rice in 1½ to 2 cups of water.

Heat the oil in a sautée pan. Add the onions and cook until soft. Add the vegetables, salt, and sugar and let the mixture simmer until the vegetables are tender, about 5 minutes. Stir only once or twice.

When the rice is cooked, transfer it to a serving dish and add the vegetables on top.

In the tadka pot, heat the oil for about a minute. When the oil is hot, add the cumin seeds, black mustard seeds, cloves, and star anise.

When the seeds begin to crackle and become fragrant, add the peanuts, cashews, dried cranberries, and raisins, stirring them gently. When the cashews start to darken slightly, add curry leaves, take it off the heat, and pour it over the rice mixture.

Garnish with chopped cilantro and serve. This dish can be made ahead of time, but add the garnish just before serving.

Anything-Goes Pilaf 

This dish is perfect for using up leftover rice and vegetables. It's similar to a Korean dish in which all the leftover foods are added to rice and topped with a sauce.

I have a habit of cooking more than I need, because I never know how much will be eaten. You can use leftover vegetables and daal too, but drain the liquid out first. If you use daal with liquid, the pilaf will be soft. The dish can be of any consistency, and you can add ingredients of your choice, including fresh vegetables like spinach to give it color. Use your imagination and add whatever your family likes. I use store bought achar masala—it adds a great zing. This recipe can be your experimental dish. There are no hard and fast rules.

The rice should have about the same volume as the rest of the ingredients put together. Yields 4 to 5 cups. Serves 4 to 6.

Ingredients:

- About 2 cups cooked rice
- About 2 cups cooked vegetables (e.g., potatoes, onions, peas, green beans)
- About 1 cup leftover daal
- About 1 cup chopped spinach (thaw first if using frozen spinach)
- ½ teaspoon salt
- ½ teaspoon achar masala

For Tadka:

- 2 tablespoons oil
- ¼ teaspoon cumin seeds
- ¼ teaspoon black mustard seeds
- 4 or 5 curry leaves
- 3 or 4 cloves
- 1 1-inch cinnamon stick or cinnamon bark
- ¼ teaspoon salt
- Pinch of turmeric powder
- 1 cup chopped nuts

The Process:

Heat oil (in a pan or skillet big enough to hold everything) at medium heat for about ½ minute.

Add thechopped nuts. Wait till they become pinkish, then add the chopped seeds and spices. When the seeds start to sizzle and crackle, add all the ingredients, starting with rice, daal, and spinach. Mix gently and let simmer for 3 to 5 minutes.

When it has the desired consistency, pour it into the serving dish. Top with yogurt and garnish with cilantro and achar spice.

Coconut Rice Pilaf 

This party favorite is quick and simple to cook but colorful and tasty. Eating just the rice cooked in coconut milk is very popular among Indian children. Yields 4 to 5 cups. Serves 4 to 6.

Ingredients for rice alone:

- 1½ cups white rice (any kind), washed and soaked
- 1 13-14 oz. can of coconut milk
- 1 cup water (for cooking)
- ¼ teaspoon salt

The Process:

Boil the water in a large pan or pot.

Add the rice and coconut milk. Partially cover and cook over medium heat for about 10 minutes.

Add the salt and sugar and simmer for another 8 to 10 minutes, until almost all the liquid has been absorbed and the rice is tender. Cover and remove from the heat.

Ingredients for Pilaf:

- 1 cup mixed vegetables, either fresh or frozen and thawed (corn, carrots, peas, and green beans)
- ½ cup chopped green onions, ¼ teaspoon salt
- 2 tablespoons fresh chopped cilantro/coriander (for garnish)

For Tadka:

- 2 tablespoons oil
- ¼ teaspoon cumin seeds
- ¼ teaspoon black mustard seeds
- 4 or 5 curry leaves
- 3 or 4 cloves
- 1 1-inch cinnamon stick or cinnamon bark
- ¼ teaspoon salt
- Pinch of turmeric powder

The Process:

Heat the oil in a large skillet.

Add the seeds, cloves, cinnamon, vegetables, curry leaves, and green onions. Stir gently.

Add the salt and turmeric and cook at low heat.

Add the cooked rice. Stir gently until thoroughly mixed. The pilaf will be light yellow. Garnish and serve.

Vermicelli Pilaf 

This dish adds variety to your pilaf by replacing the rice with vermicelli. It is easy to cook and can be made in a single pot. There is no need to soak anything. Unlike rice, this dish will not triple in volume when it is cooked. 2 cups of dry vermicelli yields 4 to 5 cups, and serves 4 to 6 people.

Ingredients:

- 1 small potato, peeled and chopped
- 1 small onion, cut into four pieces and sliced thinly
- 1 cup mixed vegetables (peas, carrots, and cut green beans)
- 2 cups vermicelli
- 1 16 oz. can of coconut milk
- 1 cup water
- 1 teaspoon (or less) salt
- ¼ teaspoon turmeric
- 2 teaspoons coriander-cumin powder (dhana-jeera mix* 1 tablespoon each chopped cilantro and grated fresh coconut)
- ¼ to ½ jalapeño or other chili pepper, chopped
- ¼ roasted cashews (for garnish)

For Tadka:

- 2 tablespoons oil
- ½ teaspoon cumin seeds
- ½ teaspoon black mustard seeds
- 4 cloves
- 4 to 5 curry leaves

The Process:

Heat the oil on medium heat in a heavy metal or nonstick pot.

Add the cumin, black mustard, cloves, and curry leaves. Let the seeds crackle and then add the potato, onion, and other vegetables and let them cook a little. Stir the mixture so that it does not burn.

Add the vermicelli and sautée it in the oil and vegetable mixture for 2 to 3 minutes. Add coconut milk and water, stirring often and gently with a wooden spoon. Reduce the heat to medium-low.

Let the dish cook for about 5 minutes, making sure that it doesn't boil over. Reduce the heat if necessary.

Add the salt, sugar, turmeric, coriander-cumin powder, and chili. Stir gently and let cook until almost all the liquid has evaporated. This dish takes 15 to 20 minutes to cook. Take it off the heat and cover it to keep it warm.

Roast the cashews in a pan, dry or with a little oil. Serve the dish warm, adding the hot cashews as a garnish. Cilantro and grated coconut can also be used as garnishes.

Soft Khicheri 

This dish is considered a comfort food, especially for the senior generation. It is also great for someone who wants soft food, and it has no spices. The original recipe used rice and mung daal with salt and turmeric, cooked until it was very soft and mushy. Ghee was added before serving, and it was served hot with kadhi (see the daal chapter). This is slightly different. Yields 4 to 5 cups. Serves 4 to 6.

This picture includes yogurt topping. For a vegan version, omit yogurt.

Ingredients:

- 1 cup medium- or long-grained rice (jasmine rice works well; basmati may not bring the same results)
- ½ cup yellow mung daal, split
- 3 to 4 cups water
- 1 teaspoons salt
- ¼ teaspoon turmeric powder
- 1 teaspoon olive oil (to add when serving)

The Process:

Wash and soak the rice and mung daal in separate bowls.

Boil 2 cups of water. Add the mung daal first and cook it for 5 minutes.

Add 1 more cup of water and the rice, salt, and turmeric. Stir gently until the salt and turmeric are mixed. Let this cook at low-medium heat for 20 to 30 minutes. Keep checking the mixture and stirring it gently every 5 minutes so that it does not stick at the bottom of the pan. Reduce the heat if needed. You may need to add more water. The cooked mixture should be soft and mushy, with the daal somewhat broken and overcooked.

This dish is generally served with yogurt or kadhi. Add ghee when serving.

This dish is considered a comfort food, especially for the senior generation.

Vegetables and Curries

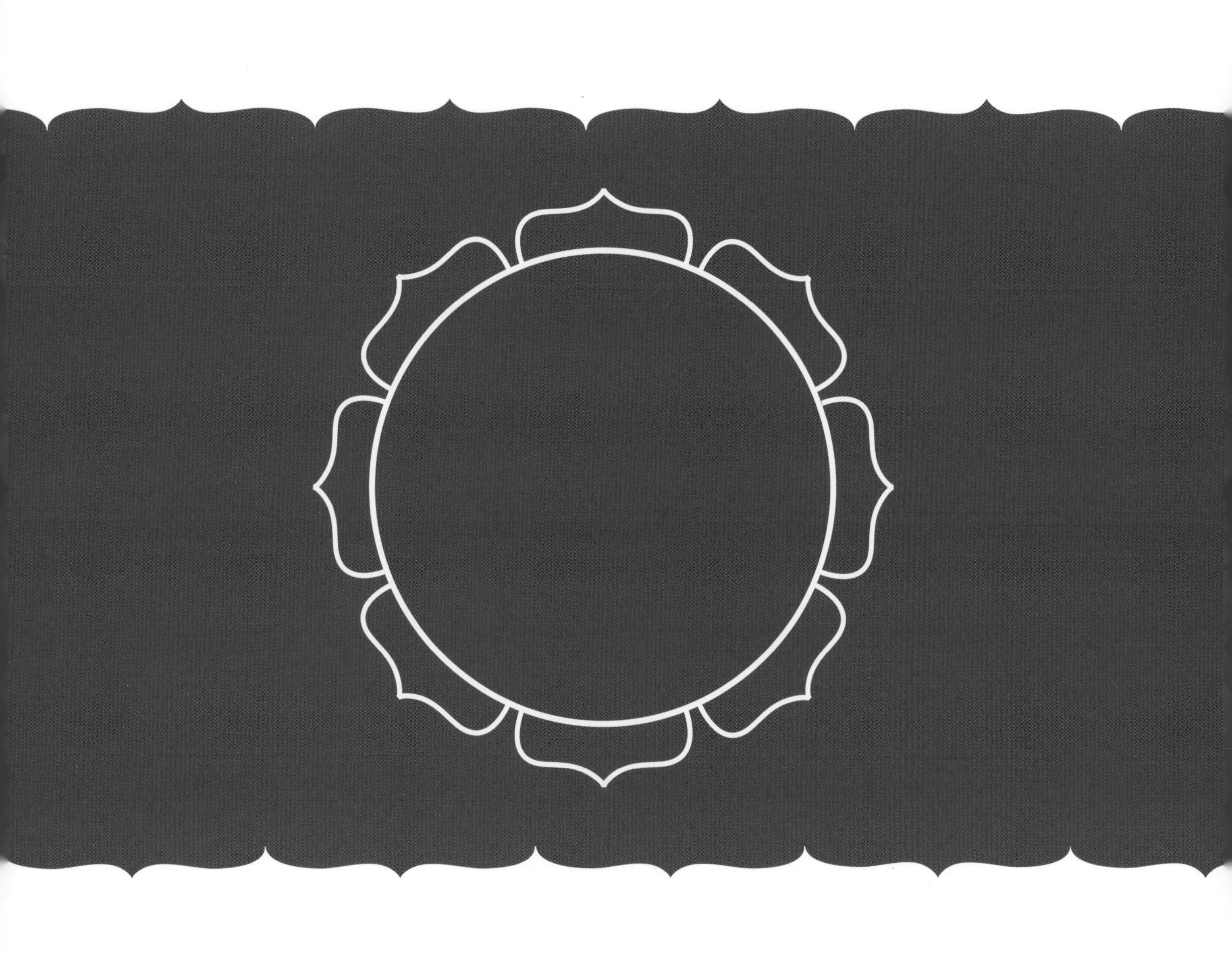

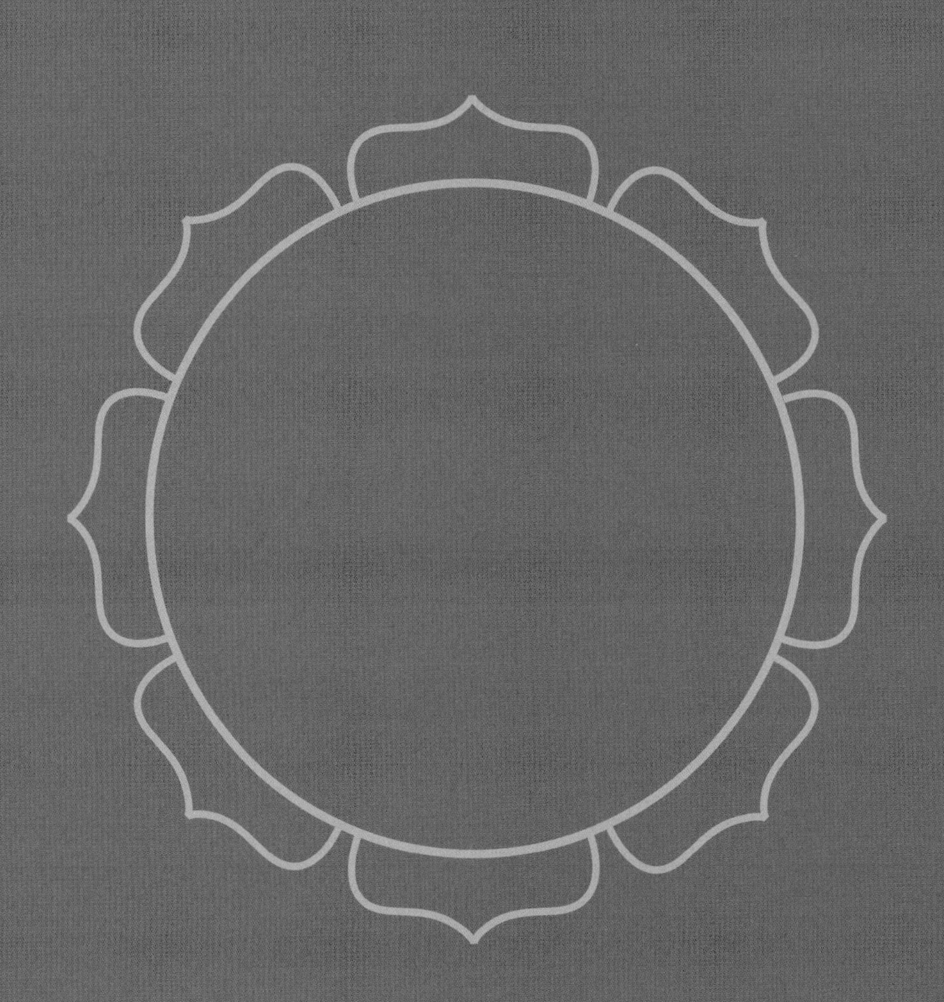

Vegetables and Curries

The most delicious part of an Indian meal is the vegetables, which can be sautéed or cooked in water. A touch of the right spices and a different cooking method can make them surprisingly tasty.

Dry and curry vegetables are served with roti and / or rice. You may find the common spices that are used with most vegetables in your spice box: turmeric, cumin, coriander powder, chili powder, cumin seeds, mustard seeds, and curry leaves. Add or subtract particular spices according to your taste. For an extra-spicy zing, add a little garam masala.

Most vegetables are cut to match the other vegetables that they will be mixed with. Choose vegetables with natural tastes and aromas that blend well, and choose spices that will enhance their flavors. Start with vegetables that take longer to cook and add the rest later. Vegetables are cut in cubes, in half-rounds or full rounds, and in long slices. The recipes often mix familiar produce like peas, green beans, cabbage, okra, spinach, eggplant, cauliflower, potato, sweet potato, carrots, spinach, and zucchini. Potatoes and peas are often added to cooked vegetables to increase volume.

Helpful tips and processes

- Do not stir vegetables very often — turn down heat so they do not stick to the bottom
- Vegetables shrink as they are cooked (especially spinach!)
- Vegetables with stems and long vegetables should have their ends cut off and vegetables with thick or rough skin should be peeled prior to cooking
- Indian vegetable dishes begin with tadka and end at the table with garnishes that depend on the dish: coconut, cilantro, chopped green chilies, or onions that are green, purple, or white
- It is a good practice to immerse vegetables in water after cutting them.
- Okra and cabbage are usually not immersed in or cooked with water. Okra can be washed in water but must be thoroughly dried before cutting
- Tadka is usually processed in the same pan in which the vegetables are cooked

This chapter will show you how to select, cut, mix, and blend vegetables and spices to make curries and other beautiful, mouth-watering dishes. Once you know which vegetables your family likes best, you can mix and match them to create your own dishes. I have used agave nectar when the vegetables are saucy.

Utensils Needed for this Chapter:

- **Many bowls to put vegetables in after cutting**
- **A colander to rinse vegetables in (if necessary)**
- **A pot to cook vegetables in**
- **A skillet (preferably nonstick) to cook vegetables in**
- **A spoon and spatula for stirring**
- **Measuring cups and spoons**
- **A chopping board and a knife**
- **Some bowls and plates to mix spices in**
- **A vegetable peeler**
- **Serving bowls and spoons**

Recipes in This Chapter

Aloo Masala (Sukhi Bhaji) 

"Aloo" means "potato." It can be made many different ways: dry, with masala, with sauce, or with other vegetables. It is okay to leave the skin on potatoes if the skin is thin and smooth. However, you may need to peel them for some dishes. Any kind of potato is okay. I use Yukon Gold or light-skinned potatoes.

Aloo masala is a favorite item for many occasions: simple to make but with a very special flavor and aroma. It can be served with any roti, paratha, or puri.

Together, aloo and puri make a great tapas dish. This dish yields about 3 to 4 cups and serves 4 to 6. If you prefer, it can be made without coconut.

Ingredients:

- 4 to 6 large potatoes, preferably white or gold
- ¼ cup grated coconut and 1 teaspoon coconut for garnish
- ¼ cup chopped cilantro + 1 tablespoon for garnish
- 1 teaspoon salt (per taste)
- 2 tablespoons coriander-cumin powder
- ½ teaspoon turmeric
- ½ teaspoon chili powder (or to taste)
- ½ teaspoon sugar
- 2 tablespoons lemon juice

For Tadka:

- 3 to 4 tablespoons oil (potatoes absorb more oil)
- 1 teaspoon panch-puran mix
- 3 to 4 curry leaves
- 1 chopped green chili (optional)

The Process:

Wash and peel the potatoes. Cut the potatoes into half-inch cubes, or cut them in half and cut into slices about ¼-inch thick. Keep them in water until ready to cook; drain just before adding to tadka oil.

Heat oil in the skillet at medium high heat for about ½ minute. Add the green chili. When the chili starts to sizzle, add the panch puran mix. When the mixture begins to sizzle / crackle, add curry leaves and drained potatoes. Add salt and stir.

Turn the heat to low medium and cook for about 7 to 10 minutes, stirring occasionally — do not cover.

Meanwhile, mix the spices, coconut, and cilantro in a bowl. Add the spices to the potatoes and mix gently until all potatoes are covered with spice mix.

Cook for another 2 to 3 minutes. Turn off the heat and cover the skillet until ready to serve.

Heat just before serving. Add lemon juice, mix gently, and garnish after putting in the serving bowl.

Aloo Rasawala 

This dish has sauce which is used like a curry. Great with any roti, paratha, or rice. Yields 4 to 5 cups and serves 4 to 6.

Ingredients:

- 4 to 6 medium potatoes, preferably white or gold, peeled and cubed
- 1½ cups water
- 2 tablespoons chopped cilantro + 1 tablespoon (for garnish)
- 1½ teaspoons salt
- 2 tablespoons coriander-cumin powder
- ½ teaspoon turmeric
- ½ teaspoon chili powder (or to taste)
- ½ agave nectar or jaggery
- 1 tablespoon tomato paste
- 2 tablespoons lemon juice (for serving)

For Tadka:

- 2 to 3 tablespoons oil
- ½ teaspoon each of mustard seeds and cumin seeds
- 3 to 4 curry leaves
- 1 chopped onion (optional)
- 1 chopped green chili (optional)
- 1 chopped tomato (optional)

The Process:

Peel and cut potatoes in small cubes. Keep them in water. Drain just before adding to tadka.

Heat oil in the pot at medium high. After about a minute, add the seeds, onions, chili, and tomato. Let the mixture simmer for two more minutes.

Add the drained potatoes and water, as well as the dry spices, salt, and sugar. Cook at medium heat for about 5 to 10 minutes.

Stir occasionally, checking to make sure there's enough water, adding any if necessary (maybe half a cup). Check whether potato is cooked by scooping out a piece and pressing it. Potato should be soft and easy to press. Add cilantro and cook for a minute.

Aloo rasawala.

Aloo mutter.

Variation 1: Aloo Mutter

To make aloo mutter, add a ½ cup of peas to the aloo rasawala recipe while cooking.

Variation 2: Aloo Bhaji

To make aloo bhaji, add 1 cup of chopped spinach to the aloo rasawala recipe while cooking.

Baingan Curry 

Many varieties of eggplant are available on the market. This dish requires long Chinese (light purple, long) eggplants, which cook fast and are easy to make. Cooking shrinks them to almost half their original size. This recipe yields about 3 to 4 cups and serves 4 to 6

Ingredients:

- 6 Chinese eggplants, each about 6 to 8 inches long
- 3 medium tomatoes, chopped
- 1 large onion, cut in half and chopped into thin slices
- 3 tablespoons coriander-cumin powder
- 1½ teaspoons ginger-chili paste
- ½ teaspoon turmeric powder
- ½ teaspoon chili powder
- ½+ teaspoon salt
- ½ teaspoon jaggery
- 1 tablespoon lemon juice (for serving)

For Tadka:

- 3 tablespoons oil
- ½ teaspoon each of cumin seeds, mustard seeds, and crushed garlic
- 3 to 4 curry leaves

Garnish:

- 3 tablespoons of cilantro

The Process:

Cut the onions and tomatoes.

For about 1 minute, heat oil for tadka in the pan you're cooking in. Add the seeds and garlic, and let the seeds simmer or crackle.

Add curry leaves, then the onions and tomatoes.

Mix and let the mixture simmer at low heat for about 5 minutes.

Meanwhile, cut the top-stems of the eggplants. Cut in half lengthwise and then cut into 2-inch pieces. Immerse in water with just a quarter teaspoon of salt.

Drain the eggplants and add to the onion-tomato mixture.

Add all the spices, salt, and jaggery, and mix gently.

Let the eggplants cook for about 5 to 7 minutes.

Just before serving, add lemon juice, mix, and top it with cilantro.

Aloo and Small Baingan Stuffed 

A little more experience in cooking vegetables will make this dish easy to follow. This dish uses Indian eggplants, or *brinjals,* and is often made for special occasions as well as for regular meals. Indian eggplants are available in many Middle Eastern and Indian markets.

Do not cut the vegetable until you have mixed the spices. Cut the tip with a knife and make two slits in eggplants and potatoes, so that they open into florets. This special vegetable dish requires slow cooking and patience. It serves 4 to 6. Cooking time is 20 minutes.

Ingredients:

- 8 Indian eggplants
- 6 medium red potatoes

Stuffing:

- 1 cup grated coconut + 1 teaspoon grated coconut for garnish
- 1 cup chopped cilantro + 1 teaspoon (for garnish)
- 3 tablespoons coriander-cumin powder
- ½ teaspoon turmeric powder
- 1 teaspoon ginger-chili paste
- 1 teaspoon chili powder
- 1 teaspoon salt (divided)
- 1 teaspoon sugar
- ¼ cup water (to be added while cooking)

For Tadka:

- 3 tablespoons oil
- ½ teaspoon each of cumin seeds and mustard seeds
- 4 curry leaves

The Process:

In a large bowl, mix coconut, cilantro, ginger-chili paste, and all spices, mixing by hand if necessary.

Wash potatoes and make crosswise slits. Immerse in about 2 cups of water.

Wash and cut stems of eggplants, make crosswise slits, and add to potatoes in water. Add about ½ teaspoons of salt (which keeps the eggplants from getting dark).

Remove the potatoes and eggplants one at a time and gently stuff them with the above mixture, then place them in another bowl. The leftover mixture will be used later.

Heat oil in a large nonstick skillet or pan. Add seeds when the oil is hot.

After about a minute, add curry leaves, take the pan off the heat, and insert the eggplants and potatoes gently into the pan.

Shake the pan slowly and gently so that the oil coats the vegetables. Add water.

Cover and cook at low medium heat, stirring gently once or twice and making sure that the vegetables do not stick at the bottom.

Add some of the mixture to the vegetables and cook until the vegetables are soft — about 15 minutes. The eggplants may change color.

Top with the rest of the spice mix and cover. Add garnish before serving.

This dish goes well with any roti, rice, and kachumber or achar.

Maharaja Special Vegetables 

This dish, a specialty of Western India, is served on special occasions. You can mix many vegetables, but the elements of the mixture must be distributed proportionately so that each vegetable can be tasted. (Give each vegetable a fair chance!) I like to use Japanese eggplant, zucchini, potatoes, yams, peas, soybeans, and green beans.

This recipe calls for a lot of cilantro and grated coconut. You can buy coconut in the frozen section of any Asian market. If unavailable, use dried unsweetened coconut from the baking section of your supermarket, soak it in warm water, and squeeze out the water.

The dish can be prepared ahead of time. When cooking vegetables, put yams and potatoes in the pot a few minutes sooner than the others, since they take longer to cook. Add sugar and salt separately to the masala mix and to the vegetables as they are cooking. Cook at low medium heat, making sure that the vegetables do not stick to the bottom. This recipe yields 6 cups and serves 6 to 8.

Ingredients:

- 1 Japanese eggplant (a thin eggplant about 6 to 8 inches long), cut in half lengthwise and then into slices 1 inch thick
- 2 medium zucchini, cut in half lengthwise and then into slices ½ inch thick
- 2 red medium potatoes, unpeeled and cut into quarters and then into slices ½ inch thick
- 1 small yam, about 4 to 5 inches long, cut into cubes ¼ inch thick
- ½ cup each of green peas (may be frozen), soybeans (shelled edamame; optional), and green beans (cut into ½ inch pieces)
- ¼ cup water
- 1 teaspoon sugar
- 1½ teaspoons salt (or to taste)
- 3 teaspoons lemon juice (for serving)

For Tadka:

- 3 to 4 tablespoons oil
- ½ teaspoon black mustard seeds
- ½ teaspoon cumin seeds
- 1 teaspoon crushed garlic (optional)
- 5 to 6 curry leaves

Masala mix:

- 2 cups grated, unsweetened coconut + 1 tablespoon of same for garnish (if you have only sweetened coconut, soak it in warm water for 5 minutes and squeeze out the water)
- 1 cup chopped cilantro + 1 tablespoon cilantro (for garnish)
- 1 teaspoon salt
- 1 teaspoon sugar
- ½ teaspoon turmeric powder
- ½ tablespoon coriander-cumin powder
- 1 teaspoon chili powder
- 2 tablespoons ginger-chili paste

The Process:

Heat oil in large nonstick pan at medium to high heat for about a minute. Add the seeds and garlic; sautée for about 2 minutes.

Add the potatoes and yam and turn the heat to medium low. Cover and cook for about 5 minutes.

Add eggplant and zucchini. Stir gently.

Add the rest of the vegetables, salt, and sugar, and about ½ cup water. Stir gently.

Cook without covering for about 5 minutes at very low heat. This will semi-cook some of the vegetables.

In the meantime, make the masala mix. Put the masala mix in a bowl and add three quarters of it on top of the vegetables. Do not stir. Let it cook uncovered for about 10 minutes, or until potatoes and yams are tender and other vegetables are cooked.

Turn off heat, stir gently, and cover. Add the rest of masala mix and lemon juice just before serving, and mix gently. Garnish with coconut and cilantro.

Baingan Bharta-Roasted Eggplant (V)

This dish requires large eggplants or baingan that are oven-roasted and the centers of which are scooped into a bowl. Since many areas of India lack ovens, baingan are often instead roasted on an open-coal fire resembling a barbeque. Messy, but tastes great.

In Middle Eastern markets, roasted eggplants are available in jars. You'll save time if you use this variety. The oven method reduces the volume. This recipe gives you the choice of either. It yields 2 to 3 cups and serves 4 to 6.

Ingredients:

- 2 large eggplant
- 1 teaspoon oil (to rub)
- ½ cup chopped cilantro (1 teaspoon for garnish)
- 2 tablespoons lemon juice
- ½ teaspoon salt or per taste
- 2 tablespoons coriander-cumin powder
- ½ teaspoon chili powder
- 1 teaspoon ginger-chili paste
- ½ teaspoon garlic, crushed or paste

For Tadka:

- 2 tablespoons oil
- 8 green onions, chopped (should make about 1 cup – save some for garnish)
- ½ teaspoon each of mustard and cumin seeds
- 1 chopped medium-sized tomato
- 4 curry leaves

The Process:

Preheat oven to roast at 400° F.

Wash and cut the eggplant in half, lengthwise. Rub oil on all sides and put the cut side down in a baking pan. Add a little oil to the pan, preferably use nonstick pan.

Bake for about 20 minutes; check whether they are soft. Meanwhile, chop the onions and tomatoes and prepare the garlic and ginger-chili paste.

Note: To make recipe vegan, remove yogurt from ingredient list.

Take the eggplant out of the oven and let cool for about 5 minutes. Hold the eggplant from the top to scoop the pulp into a bowl. Scrape any pulp still in the pan and add to the bowl. Add lemon juice right away to prevent the eggplant from turning dark.

In the cooking pot, heat oil for about half a minute.

Add seeds. Wait until they crackle, then add green onions and tomato.

Let mixture cook for about two minutes, then add curry leaves and eggplant pulp.

Add all the spices, cilantro, and pastes. Stir gently and cook at very low heat for about 5 minutes or until liquid is evaporated.

Serve warm after garnishing.

Yogurt can be added as topping or mix before serving; add salt also if necessary.

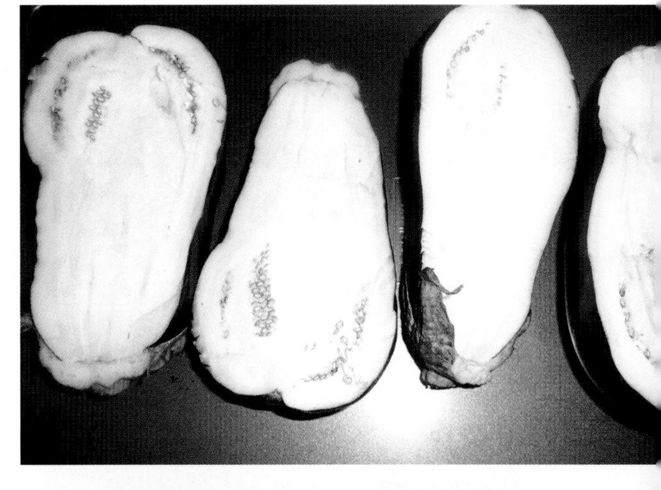

From store-bought, roasted eggplant

Note: Some Middle Eastern stores carry this item in a jar. Replace the roasted eggplant with store-bought eggplant. Drain the liquid with a sieve or a colander. Do not add salt. Cook as above, adding all other ingredients. This dish is served with millet roti, but bhakri or paratha goes especially well with it too.

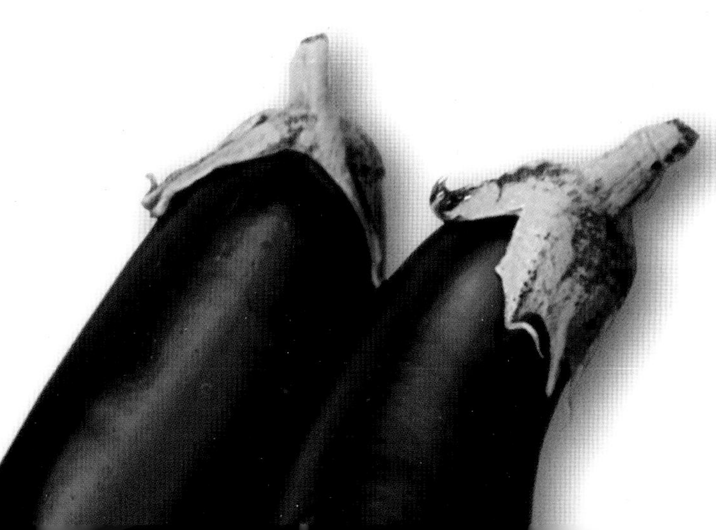

Bhendi 

Bhendi or okra is a very popular dish among Indian food lovers. It is not as popular among Western food lovers. Give it a try, though, and you may just love it. Small bhendi are tender; long ones tend to be harder. Bhendi is available in many supermarkets, produce markets, and Indian markets.

Wash before removing tips and towel dry to clean. No water is used to soak or cook this vegetable; it is cooked dry. As it is being heated, bhendi releases a sticky juice that dries up by the time it is done cooking. Salt is added only when bhendi is almost cooked. This recipe yields about 2 cups and serves 3 to 4.

Ingredients:

- 1 pound bhendi (or a little more than 2 cups)
- 1 tablespoon chopped cilantro + (1/2) teaspoon (for garnish)
- 1 tablespoon coriander-cumin powder
- ½ teaspoon chili powder
- ½ teaspoon salt (to be added last)
- ½ teaspoon lemon juice (for serving)
- ¼ teaspoon turmeric powder

For Tadka:

- 2 tablespoons oil
- ¼ teaspoon each of cumin, mustard, and fenugreek seeds

The Process:

Cut off both ends of each piece of bhendi (which reduces the volume by half), then cut the remainders into ¼- to ½-inch round pieces. Or first cut the remainders into one-inch round pieces and then into quarters by length.

This vegetable has seeds; you can place the cut bhendi in a colander so that some seeds fall out.

Heat the oil at medium heat for about half a minute.

Add seeds; when they begin to crackle, add bhendi and mix gently.

Let bhendi cook at low heat for about 7 minutes, stirring only once or twice. The bhendi will release a sticky juice that will dry once the vegetable is cooked.

Add all spices but the salt and cilantro. Bhendi may turn brown as it cooks.

Once the bhendi is dry, add salt and cilantro, stirring gently, and cook for 5 more minutes.

Garnish and serve with paratha, roti, or any flat bread.

Bhendi Masala 

This recipe is similar to the recipe for bhendi, except that now the bhendi are cut a little differently: 1½-inch sized, with a slit. This dish is made with grated coconut.

Ingredients:

- 1 pound bhendi (cut both ends and cut them to 1 inch in length; make a slit lengthwise. It's okay if some happen to get cut completely)
- ¼ cup grated coconut + 1 teaspoon (for garnish)
- ¼ cup chopped cilantro + 1 teaspoon (for garnish)
- 1 tablespoon coriander-cumin powder
- ¼ teaspoon turmeric
- ½ teaspoon salt (to be added last)
- ½ teaspoon chili powder
- 1 teaspoon lemon juice

For Tadka:

- 3 tablespoons oil
- ½ teaspoon each of mustard, cumin, and fenugreek seeds

The Process:

In a mixing bowl, mix coconut and cilantro, keeping the garnish to one side.

Add the dry spices except for the salt. Mix thoroughly – you may need to use your hands.

Take each bhendi, open the slit, and fill it with about ¼ teaspoon of the mixture. Set the stuffed bhendi on a plate.

Heat the oil and add seeds. Lower the heat and gently add the bhendi. Shake the skillet slightly so that the oil mixes with everything.

Cook for about 5 to 7 minutes, stirring gently twice.

Once the bhendi have cooked, they may turn brown; that's fine. Add salt and cook them for another 3 minutes.

Serve in a bowl after adding lemon juice and garnish.

Cauliflower 

In this recipe, the vegetables are cooked without water. The dish can also be made the way eggplant masala is made, except that the cauliflower and potatoes are cut into small pieces. This recipe yields about 3 to 4 cups and serves 4 to 6 people.

Ingredients:

- 1 medium to large whole cauliflower (about 1 to 2 pounds), cut into 1 ½-inch cubes
- 2 medium washed red or gold potatoes, cut into ½-inch cubes
- 3 tablespoons coriander-cumin powder
- ¼ cup of chopped cilantro + 2 tablespoons (for garnish)
- 1 teaspoon salt (or to taste)
- 2 teaspoons ginger-chili paste
- ½ teaspoon turmeric powder
- ½ teaspoon chili powder (or to taste)
- 1 teaspoon sugar
- 2 tablespoons lemon juice (for serving)

For Tadka:

- 3 tablespoons oil
- 1 teaspoon each of cumin and mustard seeds
- 4 to 5 curry leaves

The Process:

Cut cauliflower after removing the cover-leaves and the hard center, and immerse in water. Drain before adding to the oil.

Peel and cut potatoes and immerse in water in another bowl. Drain before adding to the oil.

Heat oil in the nonstick skillet or pan and add the seeds.

When the seeds begin to sizzle and crackle, add the curry leaves, then the drained cauliflower and drained potatoes, and mix again.

Add salt and let the vegetables cook, covered at low heat for about 10 to 15 minutes, stirring gently once or twice.

Add all the spices and most of the cilantro, leaving some for garnish.

Mix gently and cook without cover for another 5 minutes.

Just before serving, add lemon juice, mix, and garnish with cilantro.

Green Beans Masala 

Green beans or asparagus can be cut to about the same size and cooked the same way. Cooking reduces their volume. Remove the ends and cut the green beans into ½-inch pieces. Remove the tough part at the bottom of asparagus and cut into ½-inch pieces. A recipe with either base yields about 3 cups and serves 4 to 6.

Ingredients:

- 4 cups cut beans
- ½ cup grated coconut
- ½ cup chopped cilantro
- 2 tablespoons coriander-cumin powder (divided)
- ½ teaspoon salt
- ½ teaspoon sugar
- ¼ teaspoon turmeric powder
- 1 teaspoon ginger-chili paste
- 1 tablespoon lemon juice (for serving)
- ¼ cup water

For Tadka:

- 2 tablespoons oil
- ½ teaspoon each of anise seeds, cumin seeds, and mustard seeds

Garnish:

- 2 tablespoons each of grated coconut and cilantro

The Process:

Cut the vegetable and immerse in water. Drain before adding to pan.

Heat oil in the cooking pan for about a minute. Add the seeds. When seeds simmer or crackle, add your vegetable; add water, salt, and sugar; and cook uncovered at low heat for about 5 to 7 minutes.

Meanwhile, mix the coconut and all spices (but not the lemon) in a bowl.

Add the spice mixture to the vegetable and mix gently.

Cook for about 5 minutes, stirring once or twice. Keep the pot open once the contents are cooked.

Just before serving, reheat and add lemon and garnish.

Variation: Zucchini Masala

Zucchini can be cooked the same way, but the pieces should be peeled, cut lengthwise, and then cut to ½ inch long. To make this recipe use about 6 medium-sized zucchinis (5 to 6 inches long).

Green Curry (Patal Bhaji) 

In Western India, many families have this popular curry with masala puri for their Sunday dinner. You can prepare this dish ahead of time. It can be made hot or mild according to your taste. Small potatoes and pearl or tiny onions are the main vegetables used. Cooking green curry uncovered preserves the green color better.

Ingredients:

- 12 tiny potatoes, preferably red
- 12 tiny onions
- 2 to 3 cups water
- 1 cup chopped cilantro (less 2 tablespoons for garnish)
- ½ cup chopped mint
- ¼ cup fresh grated coconut (save 1 tablespoon for garnish)
- ½ cup coconut milk
- 1 teaspoon ginger-chili paste or 1 jalapeño pepper and ½ inch ginger
- 1 teaspoon crushed garlic
- 3 tablespoons coriander-cumin powder
- 2 teaspoon lemon juice (for serving)

For Tadka:

- 2 tablespoons oil
- 1 teaspoon panch puran
- 3 to 4 curry leaves

The Process:

Wash potatoes thoroughly. Immerse in water and drain just before adding to oil.

Peel onions and immerse in water. Drain just before adding to oil.

In a blender, make a paste from cilantro, coconut, mint, ginger, chili, and garlic. It doesn't need to be completely smooth, but make sure that it is a paste.

After heating oil in a pan for about a minute, add the panch puran.

When the seeds start to sizzle and crackle, add the curry leaves, drained potatoes and onions, coriander-cumin powder, and green paste.

Stir gently to coat the vegetables. Cook for about five minutes, uncovered, stirring four or five times.

Add about 1½ cups of water and salt and cook for five more minutes.

Add coconut milk and let the mixture cook, still uncovered, for another five minutes, adding water if necessary to maintain consistency of soup. The potatoes should now be soft and cooked. Remove the pot from stove.

Reheat just before serving, adding lemon juice and garnish. This dish is ideal for a large group, and it's great with rice or any paratha or puri on a cold night.

Mixed Vegetable Curry 

You must make the curry sauce first for this dish, but it can be made ahead of time and stored in a freezer for up to 3 months. Choose vegetables that give flavor and color. Serve in a soup bowl. This recipe yields about 8 cups and serves 10 to 12.

The curry sauce can be prepared separately, and yields 3 to 4 cups.

Ingredients for curry sauce:

- 4 to 6 medium onions, chopped
- 4 large tomatoes, chopped; 2 tablespoons tomato paste
- 3 tablespoons coriander-cumin powder
- 1½ teaspoons garlic paste
- 2½ teaspoons ginger-chili paste
- 2 tablespoons cashews
- 3 tablespoons oil

The Process:

Heat oil at high in a pan for a minute, add chopped onions, lower heat to medium low, and cook until the onions are soft and turning brown — about 5 minutes.

Add coriander-cumin powder and cook for 5 minutes. Add the rest of the ingredients and cook for 3 to 5 minutes. Add 2 cups of water and cook until the curry sauce shrinks a little. Remove from heat and let cool.

Place mixture in the blender, add ½ cup of water, and blend into a fine paste. This recipe makes about 3 cups.

Ingredients for vegetables:

- 2 large red potatoes, chopped
- 2 cups chopped cauliflower
- 1 cup cut green beans
- 1 can coconut milk (about 14 oz.)
- ½ cup peeled and chopped carrots
- ½ cup peas (frozen is fine)
- ½ cup chopped cilantro
- 1½ teaspoons salt (or to taste)
- 2 tablespoons coriander-cumin powder
- ½ teaspoon turmeric powder
- 1 teaspoon chili powder
- 3 tablespoons lemon juice
- 2 cups curry sauce (as prepared above)

For Tadka:

- 2 tablespoons oil
- 1 teaspoon each of cumin and mustard seeds
- 5 or 6 curry leaves

The Process:

Make sure all vegetables are immersed in water after being chopped.

Heat oil for about a minute. Add the seeds.

Once the seeds start to crackle, which takes about another minute, add the curry leaves and 1½ cups curry sauce.

Once the curry sauce heats up, add all the vegetables. Add dry spices and coconut milk.

Let the vegetables cook for about 10 minutes at low medium heat, keeping a watchful eye to ensure that the vegetables do not boil over.

Once the vegetables are cooked (are somewhat soft), turn off the heat and cover. Just before serving, add lemon juice and top with cilantro.

Street Fare

Street Fare

SNACKS AND NASHTA (TAPAS)

Indian food boasts some tasty snacks. Many of them have potatoes, either as a filler or as the main ingredient, and some use chickpea flour for a fritter batter. Most of these snacks require a chutney as a dipping sauce, and many require deep-frying or pan-frying. A lot of these snacks work like tapas —they can be meals as well. Many snack foods come with some kind of bread. These snacks are sold in stalls, and crowds gathers in the evening to eat specialties from their favorite hawkers. Every hawker has his specialty — bhel puri for some, chaat papdi or pav-vada for others, and so on. Use of chat masala and garam masala are common in these dishes.

Pakoras are made by dipping ingredients of your choice — onion, potato, eggplant, spinach, green chili — in a batter of chickpea flour and deep-frying them. Ajwain seeds are commonly used in pakoras.

Bhel puri is a mixture of puffed rice, crispy tortilla chips (home-fried), chutneys, and spices. Dahi puri is a round, crispy puffed puri filled with sprouted mung beans and chana, boiled potatoes, green and tamarind chutneys, yogurt, sav, and cilantro.

To prepare these tasty snacks at home, you should have some of these items ready: three chutneys (tamarind-date, green, and garlic); some sev (bought from the Indian market); and crispy diamond-cut fried tortillas. Almost all chutneys, and many spices that aren't used in the other chapters, will be used often in this one. The process can seem long and there are a lot of ingredients, but they are mostly chutneys, potatoes, and a few store-bought things. A visit to an Indian Market will help to know many items.

This chapter also contains recipes for various shortcuts for foods that have traditionally had very long preparation times, and recommends buying some ready-made items from the Indian market. Some of the recipes in this chapter will take longer or use many utensils.

It's best to use an oil that works well for deep-frying. My choice is grape seed oil. The beans used in this chapter have to be soaked overnight and cooked.

Utensils Needed for this Chapter:

- 6 bowls (to mix and hold ingredients)
- A deep-fryer
- Pans (to boil potatoes, mung, and chickpeas)
- A slotted spatula or spoon
- A skillet (preferably nonstick)
- A wok-style skillet
- Measuring cups and spoons
- Plates and paper linings (to hold fried items)
- A chopping board and knife
- A potato masher
- A pizza cutter
- A colander

Recipes in This Chapter

Crispy Diamond- or Square-Cut Papdi 

Making these in advance not only saves time but provides a great snack instead of chips from the packet. Flour tortillas can be purchased in any market – check the label and buy the ones without hydrogenated fat or trans fat. You can also use ready roti from Indian markets. This can be served many ways: with bhel puri, with chat papdi, or as chips with chutney. Yields about one large bag. Serves 6 to 10 people.

Note: Be watchful and careful while deep-frying. It gets easier with familiarity and practice.

Ingredients:

- 6 flour tortillas or ready roti
- 3 cups oil for frying

The Process:

Begin heating the oil in the deep-fryer at medium-high while you are cutting. Check often to be sure it doesn't overheat.

Lay one tortilla at a time on a large cutting board. Cut it at a 45-degree angle, turn the board 90 degrees, and cut again to produce diamond shapes. Squares are okay too. Pile the cut pieces in a bowl.

To check if the oil is hot enough, gently drop a cut piece in. It should float up right away. Wait a second and turn it over. It should be light brown, not dark.

Once the oil is hot enough, add a handful of the tortilla pieces and stir them gently with the spatula, turning them to fry the other side. They should take just a minute to fry. Drain the diamonds with the slotted spatula and lay them on the lined plate to absorb the oil.

Add another handful and follow the same procedure until all the pieces are fried. Turn off the heat.

When the pieces are cool, store them in an airtight container. They will keep well in the refrigerator for about two weeks and on the shelf for 7 to 10 days.

Aloo Poha (V)

This is a popular dish that's quick and easy to make and serve. It's great for when you have unexpected guests. Most households will have poha, potatoes, and onions in the pantry. Those are the main ingredients. Poha is sold in thick and thin varieties; this dish uses thick poha. Leftovers can be kept in the refrigerator and used, and reheated for two days. Serves 4 to 6 people.

Ingredients:

- 2 cups thick poha.
- 2 medium potatoes, peeled and cubed small (immerse in water after cutting)
- 1 medium onion, chopped
- 2 tablespoons cilantro, chopped (less some for garnish)
- 1 tablespoon chopped chili-ginger mix
- 1 teaspoon salt (or to taste)
- ½ teaspoon sugar
- 1 tablespoon lemon juice (for serving)
- 3 tablespoons oil
- ½ teaspoon each cumin and black mustard seeds
- ¼ teaspoon turmeric powder

The Process:

Heat the oil in the deep skillet at medium-high for about a minute. Add the cumin and mustard seeds.

When the seeds start crackling, add cloves, curry leaves, onion, and potato. Turn heat down to medium-low, cover, and let cook for 5 minutes, stirring occasionally to make sure the onions and potatoes do not burn or stick.

Wash the potatoes gently so they don't break up, soak for 5 minutes, and drain in a colander just before cooking Once the potatoes are soft and cooked, add chili-ginger, poha, salt, sugar, and turmeric powder. Mix gently with a spatula until spices are blended in and poha is soft – about 2 to 3 minutes. Add cilantro and mix gently.

Add lemon juice and mix in just before serving. Serve with green chutney for a nice spicy tangy taste.

Aloo Tiki (V)

This dish is popular during the festive season. It can be cooked ahead of time. The main ingredient is potatoes. However, please check for peanut allergy. It's important to use potatoes that are somewhat sticky when boiled; baking potatoes aren't recommended. Tapioca pearls are available in Indian markets; use the small-pearl variety. This is a pan-fried dish and is served with green or tamarind-date chutney. Makes 12 to 14 tikis.

Note: Keep some corn starch or fine cream of wheat at hand in case you need it. This is sold as sooji in Indian markets.

Ingredients:

- 4 large yellow potatoes (use Yukon Gold in the U.S.)
- ¼ cup sago (soaked in water for about 20 minutes)
- 2 tablespoons chili-ginger paste
- 1 ½ teaspoon salt
- 2 tablespoons chopped cilantro
- ½ cup coarse-ground peanuts
- ½ teaspoon ground black pepper
- 1 teaspoon roasted ground cumin
- 2 tablespoon lemon juice or ½ teaspoon citric acid
- ¼ cup oil (or as needed)

The Process:

Cut the potatoes in half and boil them at medium-high heat until soft — about 10 minutes. In the meantime, soak the sago pearls in water.

Once the potatoes are soft, drain them and add cold water or ice cubes to cool them. Peel them by hand. The skin should come right off.

Drain the tapioca pearls thoroughly. Mash the potatoes in a large bowl, then add the sago pearls, peanuts, pepper, chili-ginger paste, salt, cumin, cilantro, and

lemon juice. Mix with your hands if possible. The mixture should be soft but not pasty. Easy to work with to make patties.

Note: If necessary, add some corn starch or fine cream of wheat.

Mix well and shape into balls (about golfball sized). Press each gently to make a flat patty.

In a skillet, heat 1 tablespoon of oil over medium-low heat. When the oil and pan are hot, add one patty at a time, lining them up in the skillet. Turn heat to low, add a little oil when needed so they don't stick to the bottom.

Don't turn them until you can see that their bottoms have browned and become slightly crispy about three minutes. Then turn them one at a time with a spatula and fry the other side same way. You may need to add oil again. Remove the finished ones to a paper-lined plate.

Follow the same process until all the patties are fried. Turn off the heat.

Serve with any chutney of yourchoice of tamarind-date or green chutney.

Bombay Bondas 

This is a popular item, and most hawkers sell them with a variety of chutneys, soft bread, and other items. The main ingredient is potatoes, and the batter is made from chickpea flour. Two kinds of chutney and some fresh tomatoes and onions make this dish very popular. Makes about 12 to 14 bondas. Time: 15 to 20 minutes.

Ingredients:

- 4 to 5 large potatoes (Yukon Gold or thin-skinned varieties)
- ¼ teaspoon turmeric
- 1 teaspoon ginger paste
- 2 green chilies, minced. Adjust to taste.
- 2 tablespoons chopped cilantro
- ½ teaspoon salt (or to taste)

For Tadka:

- 2 tablespoons oil
- ½ teaspoon black mustard seeds

For Batter:

- ¾ cup chickpea flour
- 1 tablespoon chopped cilantro
- ½ teaspoon salt (or to taste)
- ¼ teaspoon turmeric
- ½ teaspoon chili powder (optional)
- ¼ cup of water
- 3 to 4 cups of oil for frying (or as needed)

The Process:

Wash the potatoes, cut them in half, and boil them with skins on until soft, about 10 minutes (check with a fork). While waiting, make the batter and ready the oil for frying.

When the potatoes are soft, drain them and put them in cold water. When they're cool, remove the skin by hand. It should peel right off.

Mash the potatoes in a large bowl. Add all the other ingredients and mix well before adding tadka.

Heat the oil for tadka. When it is hot (about 30 seconds), add the black mustard seeds and pour it over the potato mixture. Mix the potato mixture well and shape into balls slightly smaller than golf balls. Line them up on a plate.

In a separate bowl, mix the batter ingredients.

Heat the oil at medium-high. To check that it's hot enough, pour in a drop of the batter. If it floats right up, the oil is ready.

Add three to five potato balls to the batter and coat them using your hand. Drop them gently into the oil. Use the slotted spatula to turn the bondas, and cook for 4 to 5 minutes. They should be golden brown. Remove them to a paper-lined plate.

Note: Drop one ball in at a time, and drop it in gently, not from a height. First-time cooks, use a spoon to take the balls from the batter and lower them into the oil from the side. If the oil is not hot enough, the balls will sit at the bottom and break apart. If it's too hot, they won't cook properly. It takes some practice.

Serve warm with the chutney of your choice.

Variation: Pav Vada (or Vada Pav)

These are like a mini spicy potato burgers, with a little Western influence. Garnish and serve as below.

Garnish:

- ½ cup tamarind chutney
- ¼ cup cilantro chutney
- ¼ cup tomato chutney or 1 thinly sliced tomato (optional—sometimes I use salsa)

Serving:

Warm the buns and cover them with cloth. Slit each bun in half and spread cilantro chutney and tamarind chutney on each side — ½ to 1 teaspoon.

Place a bonda on one side and top with a slice of tomato or tomato chutney. Put the other side on, and you have a Bombay pav vada, or a mini potato burger.

BOMBAY BONDAS

PAV VADA

Bhel Puri (V)

This is one of the most popular snacks and meals in many major Indian cities. It requires three chutneys, beans, potatoes, and some items readily purchased in an Indian market. Bhel puri is a mixture of puffed rice, small crispy puris, and sev. It may seem strange at first to use puffed rice, but all the other ingredients make it taste very different.

Note: Mung and chickpeas are optional. If used, they should be soaked overnight and boiled until cooked. Sprouted tastes very nice. Advance planning and preparation are helpful. Chutneys can be made ahead of time and frozen. Beans will add some protein. This a dish in which you can use more items to make it different and make it your own way. It's ideal as a snack, lunch, or dinner on warm summer days. It's also a favorite party dish.

This dish uses many bowls to serve, and setting the table is very important. Once you have the table set, show your guests how to mix and serve as below. Serves 8 to 10 people.

Ingredients:

- 1 packet bhel puri mix (Indian markets sell these in 2-pound and 5-pound sizes. Use the 5-pound package. This mixtures stays well in the refrigerator for months)
- 1 cup boiled sprouted mung beans, sprouted, cooked (optional)
- 1 cup boiled sprouted chickpeas, sprouted, cooked (optional)
- 4 potatoes, boiled, peeled, and cut into small cubes
- 2 to 3 cups tamarind-date chutney
- 1 cup green chutney, with ½ cup water added
- ½ cup garlic chutney (add a little water if needed)
- 2 medium purple onions, chopped
- 1 cup chopped cilantro
- 1 cup pomegranate seedlings (when in season — optional)
- 1 cup chopped tomatoes
- 2 cups sev (purchased from Indian market)
- 1 lemon, cut in 8 pieces
- Salt, chili powder, and chat masala to sprinkle on top

The Process:

Put all items in separate bowls, with bhel puri mix in a large one. This makes a great spread.

Serve: This is the fun part of this dish.

In a soup dish or deep bowl, add 1 cup of bhel puri mix, then mung, chickpeas, potatoes, onions, and tomatoes, a tablespoon or less each. Add 3 to 4 tablespoons of the tamarind-date chutney and about a teaspoon of the other chutneys. Mix gently with a spoon.

Add cilantro, and garnish with 1 teaspoon or more sev, and pomegranate seedlings. Add lemon and spice it to taste by adding chutneys and masalas. Once you make one plate, you will know what to use more or less of.

Chat Papdi 

This is a colorful and delicious chat with spicy potato mix and garbanzo beans. It's a wonderful starter or snack. It's served as a starter in many restaurants and is a popular dish at parties and gatherings. This dish requires chutneys, yogurt, and many colorful items. Get everything ready first and make a plateful when ready to serve. Serves 6 to 8.

Ingredients:

- 2 cups diamond or square papdi
- 2 potatoes, boiled and mashed
- 1 can garbanzo beans, washed and drained
- ½ cup sev purchased from an Indian store
- ½ cup tamarind-date chutney
- ½ cup cilantro chutney
- 2 tablespoons pomegranate seeds (when in season)
- ½ cup chopped onions and chopped cilantro
- ½ cup chopped tomato
- 1 teaspoon each chat masala and chili powder

Arranging the Papadi and Garnishing:

Mix the potatoes with cilantro chutney.

Place the papdi in one layer on a flat large serving plate. Place the spicy potato mixture on top. Add a layer of garbanzo beans. Pour on the tamarind-date chutney. Pour yogurt over it. (The chutney and yogurt are for taste and should not cover it entirely.) Add onions and tomatoes in another layer. Put pomegranate seeds on top (optional). Add sev in another layer. Top with cilantro and sprinkle with chat masala and a little chili powder. Add yogurt if desired.

Dahi Puri

This appetizer is easy to serve once you have all the ingredients ready. Most of them are similar to bhel puri, except the pani puris, which are puffed crispy puris, are used as the main ingredient. This is a popular hawker dish and is prepared at the time of serving. These puris are time-consuming and difficult to make at home. They are available at Indian markets in boxes of 25 or 50. If you are totally new at this, use the smaller amount. Once you have mastered the art of preparing them, you can invite friends to show off your creations. Serves 4 to 5, about 25 puris.

Ingredients:

- Pani puri, box of 25, store-bought
- 3 medium potatoes, boiled, skinned, and chopped or mashed
- 1 cup tamarind-date chutney
- 1 cup yogurt + ½ cup milk + ½ teaspoon salt whisked smooth
- ½ cup green chutney
- ½ cup whole mung, soaked overnight and boiled (optional)
- ½ cup chickpeas, soaked overnight and boiled (optional)
- ¼ cup chopped cilantro
- ¼ cup sev (purchased from Indian market)
- 1 teaspoon or less chat masala
- ¼ teaspoon salt
- 1 pinch each salt, chili powder, chat masala, roasted ground cumin

The Process:

Mix the potatoes with cilantro chutney. Cut potatoes in small cubes. Drain boiled mung and chickpeas separately. Whisk yogurt and add ¼ teaspoon salt.

How to serve:

Put all items in separate bowls, using sizes that fit each amount. Line up puris on a plate (small if serving only yourself, large if serving guests). With the back end of a fork or spoon, gently make ½-inch holes in each puri. (It's okay if they are larger. Some puris may break, and it's okay to use them.)

Fill these puris (or, if broken, top them) in this order: First, 2 to 3 small pieces of potato; second, a little mung and chickpeas.

Pour a little green chutney on each, ¼ teaspoon or less. Pour yogurt on each but do not cover fully. This is for taste. Pour on the tamarind-date chutney. All the puris should have some of the yogurt and the chutney. Sprinkle cilantro and sev over them and a little chat masala. Add a final touch by sprinkling on a little salt and chili powder.

Use a flat spoon or pie server to serve. Add to each extra yogurt and chutney from the serving plate.

Pakoras—Spinach, Onion, and Jalapeño 

Pakoras (fritters) are popular as snacks and starters at parties. When the batter is ready, you can use many items of your choice. This recipe calls for green chilies, onions, and spinach. Pakoras are served with chutneys as a dipping sauce. Makes 4 to 6 cups of pakoras. Serves 6 to 8 as a starter.

Batter:

- 2 cups chickpea flour
- 2 tablespoons rice flour
- ½ teaspoon salt
- ½ teaspoon baking soda
- Pinch of ajvain (like anise seeds)
- Pinch of turmeric powder
- ½ cup or a bit more water

In Separate Bowls:

- 1 cups spinach leaves, washed, stems removed, and chopped
- 1 large onion, cut in quarters and sliced
- 2 green chili peppers (such as jalapeños) cut lengthwise, seeds removed, and sliced round
- 3 to 4 cups oil for frying

The Process:

Make the batter in a bowl, then cut the vegetables and put them in another. Heat the oil in a deep-fryer at medium-high, and keep close watch on it. The oil should be hot in 5 to 7 minutes. To check if it is hot enough, add a drop of the batter using a spoon. It should float right up.

Fry one item at a time. Place the pakoras on a plate with a chutney bowl in the middle to serve.

Uttapam

This popular South Indian dish takes very little time to prepare. Many South Indian dishes require soaking rice and urad daal and grinding. This is a quick version. It's made like a pancake. You can make a single large one for a great meal, or many small ones as starters. I've often seen large uttapams sliced like pizzas. This dish is served with coconut or tomato chutney. The main ingredient is sooji, farina, or cream of wheat, which is sold in Indian and Middle Eastern markets. Makes 3 or 4 large pieces or 6 to 8 small ones, and serves 3 to 4.

Note: Sometimes the first one breaks apart. This means that the skillet was too hot.

Ingredients:

- 1½ cups fine (not coarse) sooji
- ½ cup plain yogurt
- 1 cup warm water
- 1 teaspoon salt
- 1 teaspoon ginger-chili paste
- ½ teaspoon soda
- 1 onion, chopped
- 4 curry leaves, chopped
- 2 tablespoons chopped cilantro
- ½ cup oil (approximate)
- ½ cup coconut chutney

For Tadka:

- 1 tablespoon oil
- 1 teaspoon urad daal
- ½ teaspoon black mustard seeds

The Process:

Mix all dry items and add yogurt and water. Whisk until smooth. Let stand for 10 minutes. You may need to add water — the mixture should be like pancake batter.

Heat oil in tadka pan. Add urad daal and mustard seed. When the daal changes color, remove and add to the above mixture.

In the meantime, prepare a plate for the uttapam, a small bowl of oil, a teaspoon for adding oil to the pan, and a spatula.

Heat the nonstick pan over medium heat. Check with a drop of water that the pan is hot but not extremely hot. Add a teaspoon of oil and pour about ¼ cup of the mixture into the pan, letting it spread out like a pancake. Add a little more oil on side, and let it cook until the top bubbles, 3 to 5 minutes.

Turn it over with a spatula. The bottom side should be light brown. Let it cook again for another 3 to 5 minutes.

Serve with coconut chutney.

Chutney Sandwich

This is a popular finger food sold by many street vendors. There is some variety in the way it's made, so take your pick: plain chutney sandwich, or chutney sandwich with tomato and cucumber. One loaf of bread will make sandwiches for many people. You can make them full-size or quarter-size. The chutney you use depends on how hot you like your food. Add a little cream cheese or Greek yogurt to make it milder. This recipe makes four full-sized square sandwiches or sixteen quarter sandwiches—great finger food. It also makes a great appetizer.

Ingredients:

- 8 slices of your favorite bread, crusts trimmed off
- 2 tablespoons green chutney
- 1 tablespoon Greek yogurt or cream cheese
- 1 teaspoon butter, softened
- 16 thin slices of tomatoes (optional)
- 16 thin slices of cucumber (optional)
- Salt and pepper to taste (use with tomato and cucumber)

The Process:

Take any bread you like that comes in square slices, and trim the crusts off. Butter each slice on one side. Spread the chutney mix on each slice. Top one side with tomato and cucumber slices, sprinkle a little salt on them, and put the chutney side of the other slice on top. Gently press and then cut to the size you like: Leave it whole, or cut it in half or in quarters, long or square.

These can be made ahead of time and served with your favorite drink.

Sweets and Desserts

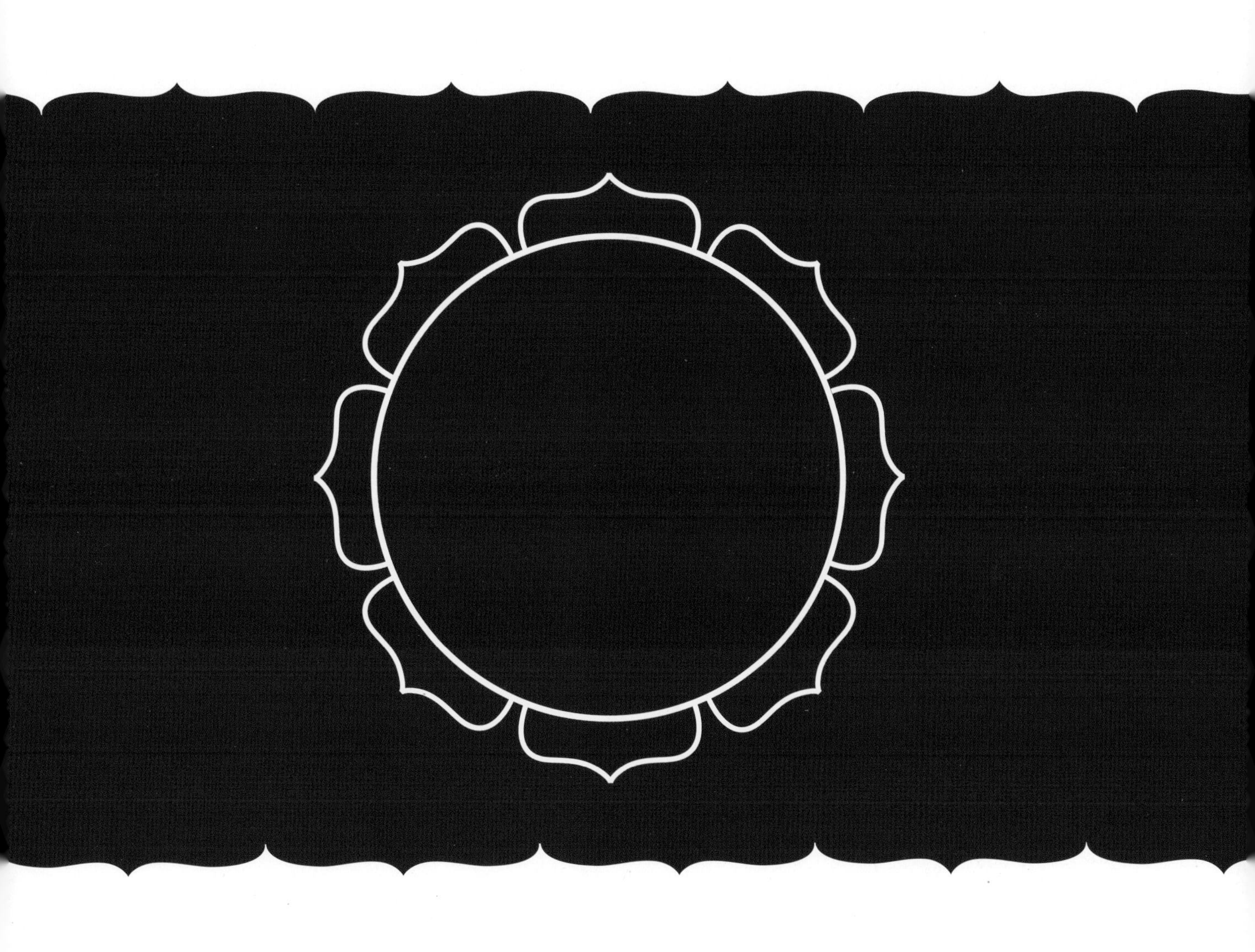

Sweets and Desserts

Indian sweets come in many different colors and textures. They differ from most American desserts in their base ingredients. Most are made with milk, mava (a thickened milk somewhat like ricotta cheese), ghee (clarified butter), chickpea flour, cream of wheat, semolina noodles, carrots, rice, and cashew, almond, or pistachio powder, among other things. All of this is in addition to flour (wheat and bulgur wheat) and, of course, sugar. Many varieties of nuts are also used in making Indian sweets.

They also differ in preparation. Most Western sweets are baked in the oven, but the majority of Indian desserts are made in a pan on the stovetop. Sweet dishes are also garnished with crushed or blanched almonds and crushed pistachios. Some sweets include cashews, cardamom, saffron, raisins, dates, and walnuts.

Many kinds of sweets are sold in Indian markets and restaurants. It's best to try a little first, though, as they are very sweet indeed. The Indian sweet stores will display varieties of colors, sizes, shapes and styles of sweets during the festival season. Typical sweets are jalebi, peda, ladoo, colorful bars, mathari, gulab jamuns, and countless other items

This chapter gives time-saving recipes for many mouthwatering traditional delicacies that normally take a long time to prepare, including carrot halva (a carrot cake with chopped nuts and raisins), falooda (a dessert drink made with milk, flavored syrup, ice cream, noodles, and takmari), black basil seeds (chia seeds), kheer-rice pudding (flavored with cardamoms and saffron and topped with crushed nuts), and gulab jamuns (dumplings made with milk powder).

In India, sweets were traditionally served as accompaniments to the main dishes. Today, however, Western influence has prevailed and most families serve desserts after the main course.

Utensils Needed for this Chapter:

- Heavy duty pans with lids
- Skillets – nonstick preferred
- Many different-sized bowls
- Pie plates or plates with raised edges
- Knives, spoons, bowls
- A deep-fryer and a slotted spatula
- A nonstick spatula and spoons
- Plates to put prepared items
- Measuring cups and spoons
- Shredder
- An ice cream scoop
- A whisk
- A chopper

Recipes in This Chapter

All milk-based sweets should be refrigerated after use.

Payasam, Sevia or Sev-Kurma

This dish is known as "sevia" or "sev-kurma" in North India and as "payasam" in the South. It can be served warm in the cold season and cold in the hot season. It is made from very thin semolina vermicelli noodles, milk, sugar, nuts, and a touch of saffron. It is usually served with a meal but can also be served as dessert afterward.

Traditionally, the noodles are sautéed in ghee (Indian clarified butter), but you can buy pre-roasted vermicelli at Indian grocers, where the long, thin noodles are sold in plastic packets. Before cooking, gently crush the vermincelli in the closed packet into pieces about 1 inch long.

Saffron gives this dish its vibrant color and flavor, but you only need a few strands. Don't use too much. The color is very intense.

This recipe makes enough to serve five or six people and will last two or three days in the refrigerator. It can be served warm or cold.

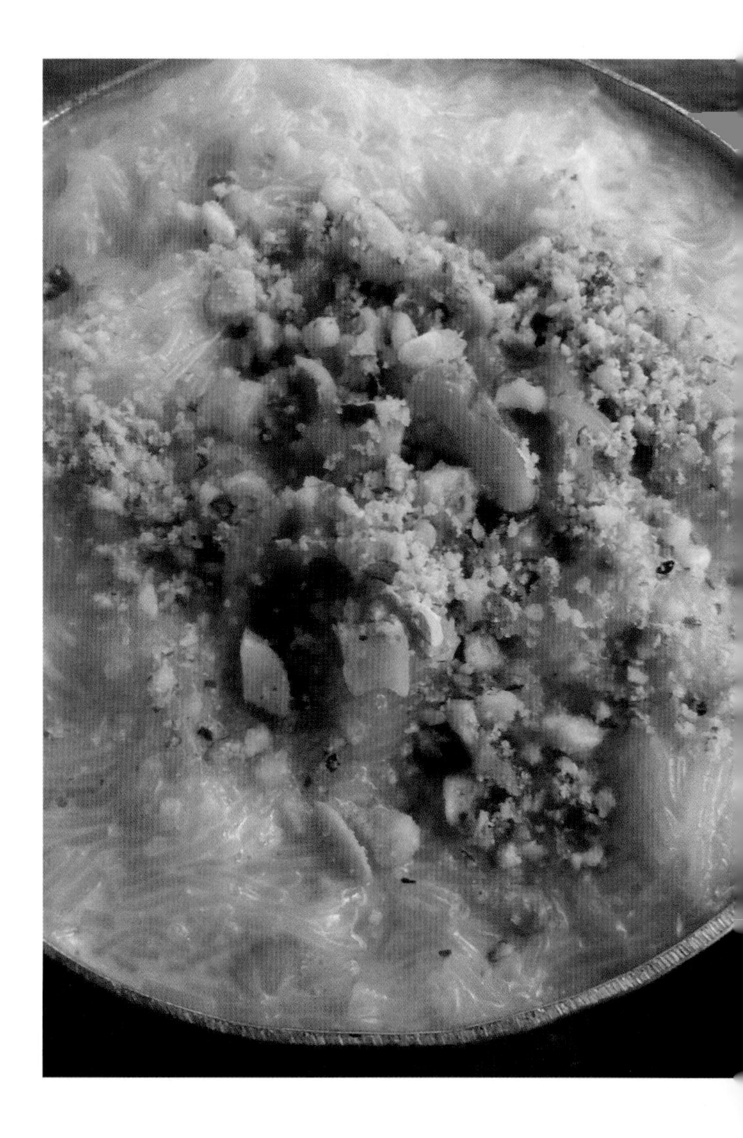

Ingredients:

- 1 cup roasted vermicelli, hand-crushed
- 1 cup water
- 1 to 1½ cups milk
- 3 tablespoons sugar (or slightly less)
- 1 cup + 2 tablespoons of any combination of raisins, chopped cashews, sliced almonds,

For Garnish:

- 4 to 5 strands of saffron
- 2 tablespoon crushed nuts

The Process:

Put the vermicelli in the water and let soak for 5 minutes, then bring to a boil.

Turn off stove and cover. Let stand for 5 to 7 minutes. Add milk. Stir to make sure there are no lumps. Bring to a boil over low to medium heat.

Stir once or twice to mix the vermicelli and prevent it from becoming lumpy.

Add sugar. Simmer, stirring, for 5 to 7 minutes. Add nuts and raisins, stir gently, and cover. Remove from heat let sit 5 minutes.

Serve warm in bowls, and add saffron to garnish. Cover to prevent it from developing skin on top, and for saffron to release the color and flavor.

Gulab Jamun

Gulab jamun is easily the most popular and beloved dessert in India. Think of it as an Indian version of sweet dumplings. This recipe makes 16 dumplings and serves 6 to 8 people. Preparation time: 15 minutes. Cooking time: 20 minutes.

Ingredients:

- 1 cup nonfat milk powder
- ¼ cup all-purpose flour
- a small pinch of baking soda
- ½ cup heavy cream, as needed
- ¼ teaspoon cardamom, coarsely ground

For Frying:

- About 3 to 4 cups oil

For Syrup:

- 1½ cups sugar
- 1½ cups water

The Process:

For syrup: Add water and sugar to a pan, bring to boil, and stir until the sugar dissolves. Turn the heat off and set the pan aside.

For gulab jamun: In a large mixing bowl, mix the milk powder, flour, baking soda, and cardamom. Add cream and mix well. The dough should have a very soft consistency and stick easily to the fingers. If it feels very dry, add 1 or 2 spoonfuls of milk (not the cream). As the dough sits, the milk powder will absorb the extra cream. Cover and set aside for about 10 minutes.

Grease your palms with ½ teaspoon of oil, and then knead the dough. Use more oil if needed. Divide the dough into 18 equal parts and roll them into balls.

Put at least 1 inch of oil in a frying pan and heat at medium. To test the oil's temperature, put a small piece of dough in it; the oil should sizzle, but it should take about 30 seconds for the dough to rise. If it rises faster, the oil is too hot; if it just sits without rising, the oil is not hot enough. Heat oil to medium high.

Place the gulab jamun in the deep-fryer. They will increase in size, so be sure to give them enough space. Fry them for about 3 to 5 minutes. While the first batch is frying, keep making gulab jamun balls. You can make them in different sizes and shapes. Fry until the gulab jamuns are brown.

Let the balls cool off for a few minutes before placing them in the hot (not boiling) syrup. Let the gulab jamuns sit in the syrup for at least 20 minutes before serving.

Additional Tips: **If the gulab jamuns are fried on high heat, they will become hard inside and not be fully cooked.** Too much baking soda will make the gulab jamuns too soft or cause them to break up when frying. Don't put the gulab jamuns in the syrup immediately after frying. This will make them lose their shape and turn chewy.

Coconut Almond Bars 

These are easy to make and delicious. They are also vegan and gluten-free. This recipe serves 4 to 6 people.

Ingredients:

- 2 cups coconut, freshly grated (I use frozen shredded coconut)
- ½ cup sugar
- ½ cup almond powder
- ¼ teaspoon cardamom powder

The Process:

Add coconut and sugar to a nonstick frying pan and cook over medium-low heat, stirring continuously until the sugar is melted and the mixture starts to bubble.

Add the almond powder and cardamom and keep stirring, scraping the sides and bottom of the pan, until the mixture starts coming together and takes on the consistency of soft dough. This should take 6 to 7 minutes. Turn off the heat.

Pour the mixture into a greased plate while still hot and spread it evenly, about ¾ inch thick. Press with a spatula to make it firm. While the mixture is still warm, cut it into one-inch squares.

Allow to cool for about an hour until it is dry and holds its shape. Then remove the bars from the plate. They can be stored up to one week in an airtight container.

Note: To blanch almonds, drop them in boiling water for five minutes, then drain and rinse under cold water. Press the almonds one by one and squeeze the skin lightly to pop. Slice and use the almonds as topping to sweets.

These are easy to make and delicious. They are also vegan and gluten-free.

Basen Ladoos

Basen ladoos are rich, sweet dessert-snacks made from gently roasted chickpea flour. They can be served any time of the day. In Indian households, ladoos are traditionally served as cookies and chocolates. They can be made gluten-free — just don't add the semolina. This recipe makes about 16 ladoos and serves 6 to 8 people.

Ingredients:

- 1½ cups chickpea flour (also called "basen")
- 2 tablespoons fine semolina (sooji) or cream of wheat
- 2 tablespoons almond powder
- ½ cup unsalted melted butter (ghee)
- ¾ cups sugar
- 4 tablespoons sliced almonds
- ¼ teaspoons coarsely-ground cardamom seeds

For Garnish:

- 1 tablespoon sliced pistachios

The Process:

Put the chickpea flour, semolina, and butter in a large pan and mix.

Turn the heat to medium and roast the mixture until light golden brown. Stir continuously with a spatula to prevent burning. When the color has changed you will also start to smell the sweetness of roasted basen. This should take 7 to 10 minutes. *Note:* Cooking on high heat prevents the mixture from cooking fully.

While the mixture is warm, add the cardamom seeds, almonds, and sugar, and mix. Let the mixture cool. If you make ladoos with a warm mixture, they will flatten.

To make the ladoos, put 1 tablespoon of the mixture into your palm. Gently press it between your palms to form a smooth, round ball. They are usually the size of a golfball, but you can adjust them as you prefer.

Put ladoos back on the plate. Top with pistachios, and press them in a little.

Let the ladoos cool to room temperature and then put them in a covered container. They can be stored in an airtight container for up to 2 weeks.

Refrigeration not required.

Kheer

Kheer is an Indian version of rice pudding cooked with milk and sugar and flavored with nuts and saffron. This recipe makes about 4 cups and serves 4 to 6 people.

Ingredients:

- 1 cup rice
- 1 cup water
- 2 cups whole milk
- ¼ cup sugar (or to taste)
- 6 strands saffron
- A pinch of crushed cardamom
- 2 tablespoons sliced almonds
- 1 tablespoon sliced pistachios
- 1 tablespoon golden raisins

The Process:

Rinse the rice, changing the water until it stays clear.

Add the water and milk and cook until the rice is tender and the milk is creamy and reduced to about half. Stir often to ensure the milk does not burn.

Add the sugar, saffron, cardamom, almonds, and pistachios, and let simmer for a few more minutes. Turn off the heat. As the kheer cools it will thicken in texture. It can be served warm or chilled.

Refrigerate after use; stays well for 2 to 3 days.

Carrot Halva

This dish has a lot of nutrients, as it is made from carrots, milk, and cheese. It can be served cold in summer and warm in winter. This recipe is different from others, as I use ricotta cheese instead of just milk. Is very simple and easy to make. This recipe makes about 3 cups and serves 4 to 6 people.

Ingredients:

- 4 cups peeled and shredded carrots
- 2 tablespoon ghee or unsalted butter
- 1½ cup ricotta cheese
- 1 cup milk
- 1 cup sugar
- ½ cup golden raisins, washed and drained
- ½ cup chopped nuts

The Process:

Heat the ghee or butter at low heat until it melts, then add carrots and stir gently.

Let the carrots cook in the ghee for 3 minutes. Add milk and cook for 5 minutes or until the milk is evaporated.

Add sugar and ricotta. There will be liquid from them. Stir gently to make sure that the mixture does not stick to the sides and that the carrots do not break up.

Cook until the mixture is thickened. Turn off the heat, add raisins and cover. Mix the raisins and add chopped nuts in, and serve.

Refrigerate after use; stays well for 2 to 3 days.

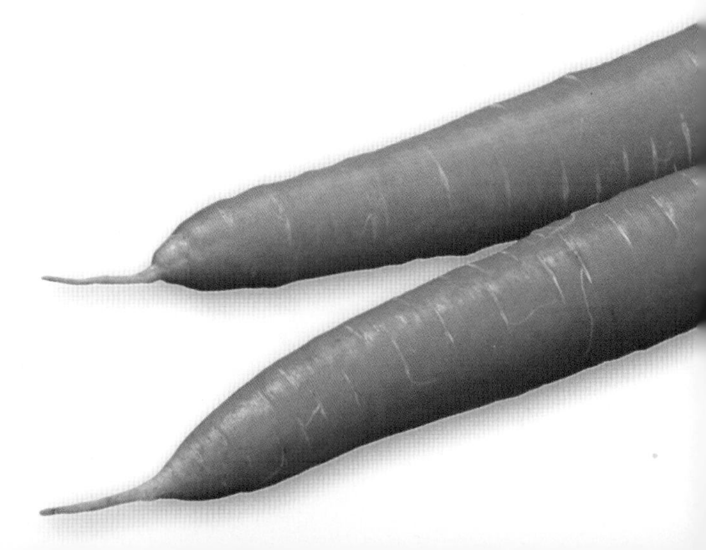

Welcome-Home Lapsi

Lapsi is considered a welcome-home dish. It is made for special occasions, such as moving to a new home, someone visiting home, or any other happy event. It's easy to make and does not need continuous attention and stirring, and it is very wholesome.

This dish is made with cracked wheat, also known as "fada" in Indian markets and "bulgur wheat" in Middle Eastern markets. This grain is not wheat germ, but it looks like it. Until recently, ghee was used to roast the fada, but now oil is used most often. The volume increases about three times when it is cooked.

Ingredients:

- 1 cup cracked wheat
- 1/3 cup ghee or oil
- 1 cup sugar
- 3 to 3½ cups water.
- ½ cup blanched or sliced almonds
- ½ cup golden raisins
- ½ cup water
- A few strands of saffron

The Process:

Heat oil in the pan at medium-low heat and add the cracked wheat, stirring often until the wheat changes color and you can smell its aroma. Add the water and sugar and stir until the sugar is melted. Turn the heat to low, cover the pan, and cook for about 30 minutes undisturbed. Then check to see that all the water has evaporated. Add raisins and cover.

To add color, drop a few strands of saffron into ½ cup of water, and soak the sliced almonds in it for few minutes. Take them out and let them dry. Add the saffron water to the cooked lapsi and mix.

Serve the lapsi in a bowl and sprinkle almonds on top. To make it colorful, you can soak the sliced almonds in food colors, then drain and garnish.

Shiro or Halwa

This dish is made from semolina, also known as "farina" or "cream of wheat." It is made for special purposes, and many folks take it to their place of worship. Regardless, it is also a very popular sweet dish in many regions of India. It's easy to make and uses milk and nuts.

Ingredients:

- 1 cup semolina
- 2½ cups warm milk
- 1 cup sugar
- ½ cup ghee or oil
- ½ cup chopped almonds, golden raisins, chopped pistachios
- 2 teaspoon milk, with 4 or 5 strands of saffron added to it

The Process:

Warm the milk and keep it covered.

Put the ghee in a round frying pan, preferably nonstick. Add the semolina and stir gently until it is light pink and you can smell the aroma.

Add the milk — be extra careful to avoid splattering, and stir gently so no lumps are formed. Put on low heat, stirring often so the mixture does not stick to the bottom. The semolina will increase in volume as it cooks. Cook it until all the liquid has evaporated.

Add sugar and mix. The mixture will be watery. Cook until all the liquid is gone again. The mixture should stir easily.

Add raisins and cover for about 10 minutes.

Before serving, add the saffron mixture and mix. This dish can be heated in the microwave if necessary. Serve it warm, garnished with chopped almonds and pistachios.

Shrikhand with Saffron and Nuts

This dessert is the original version of Greek yogurt. It's served on many occasions, especially weddings, festivals, and other parties. It can be served in individual bowls or as needed.

Shrikhand is made by the same process as Greek yogurt: Put plain yogurt in a fine muslin cloth lining a bowl, tie the muslin at the top, and hang it for 4 to 6 hours to let the water drain. You can also use the Greek yogurt you buy in markets, but it might need more sugar, as it can be a little sour. This dish can be made plain with sugar, and garnished with saffron and chopped nuts or with fruits and nuts. Flavored Greek yogurt can also be used. This makes a great dessert. Serve it cold. It makes enough for 6 to 8 people.

To make Greek yogurt, please refer to page 193.

Ingredients:

- 1 quart of Greek yogurt
- 3 tablespoons of powdered sugar (or agave nectar)
- 2 tablespoons milk, with 10 to 12 strands of saffron added
- ¼ cup chopped almonds and pistachios
- ½ teaspoon crushed cardamom

The Process:

Put the Greek yogurt in a deep mixing bowl, whisk to remove any lumps, add sugar and mix with a spatula until the sugar is mixed well.

Add the saffron mixture and mix until the color is even.

Sprinkle with cardamom and chopped nuts just before serving.

This dessert is the original version of Greek yogurt. It's served on many occasions, especially weddings, festivals, and other parties.

Falooda

This dessert is a great item to serve instead of just ice cream. Once you make it, your guests will want it every time. Many ingredients are needed to make this popular dish. Some of the ingredients are uncommon but can be found in Indian markets. You need to buy takmaria (black chia seeds, sometimes known as basil seeds) and falooda sev. I have used bean threads from Asian markets, which work great. Ice cream syrup (flavored sugar syrup) is also available in Indian markets.

Prepare the items ahead of time and serve when ready. It's easy to have everything ready in bowls except the ice cream. I use the green jello available in cans in Asian markets (or optionally mint jello). You can add chopped nuts or colorful fruit to make it your own creation. Serve it in small clear glasses. This recipe serves 6 people.

Ingredients:

- 3 cups milk
- ½ gallon vanilla ice cream
- 2 cups crushed ice
- 3 tablespoons ice cream syrup
- 1 small packet falooda sev
- 3 teaspoons takmaria seeds
- About 1 dozen strands of falooda sev or bean threads
- 3 tablespoons chopped almonds

The Process:

Soak the takmaria in a cup of water. They will puff up with a translucent coating within 10 minutes.

Soak the falooda sev in 1½ cups water for 10 minutes and then boil for 10 minutes and drain. Cut them into 2-inch pieces and keep in a covered bowl.

Open both sides of the green jello can and remove it to a flat dish. Slice some and chop them into about ½-inch pieces (this is optional). Mint jello can be used if green jello is not available.

Serving:

Use six small glasses. In each one, put ½ cup milk and crushed ice, then top with two scoops of ice cream. Pour a teaspoon of syrup on top of each.

Add falooda sev strands — about 6 strands each. Add takmaria and top with almonds. Fruits like strawberries can also be added for color.

Everything Else

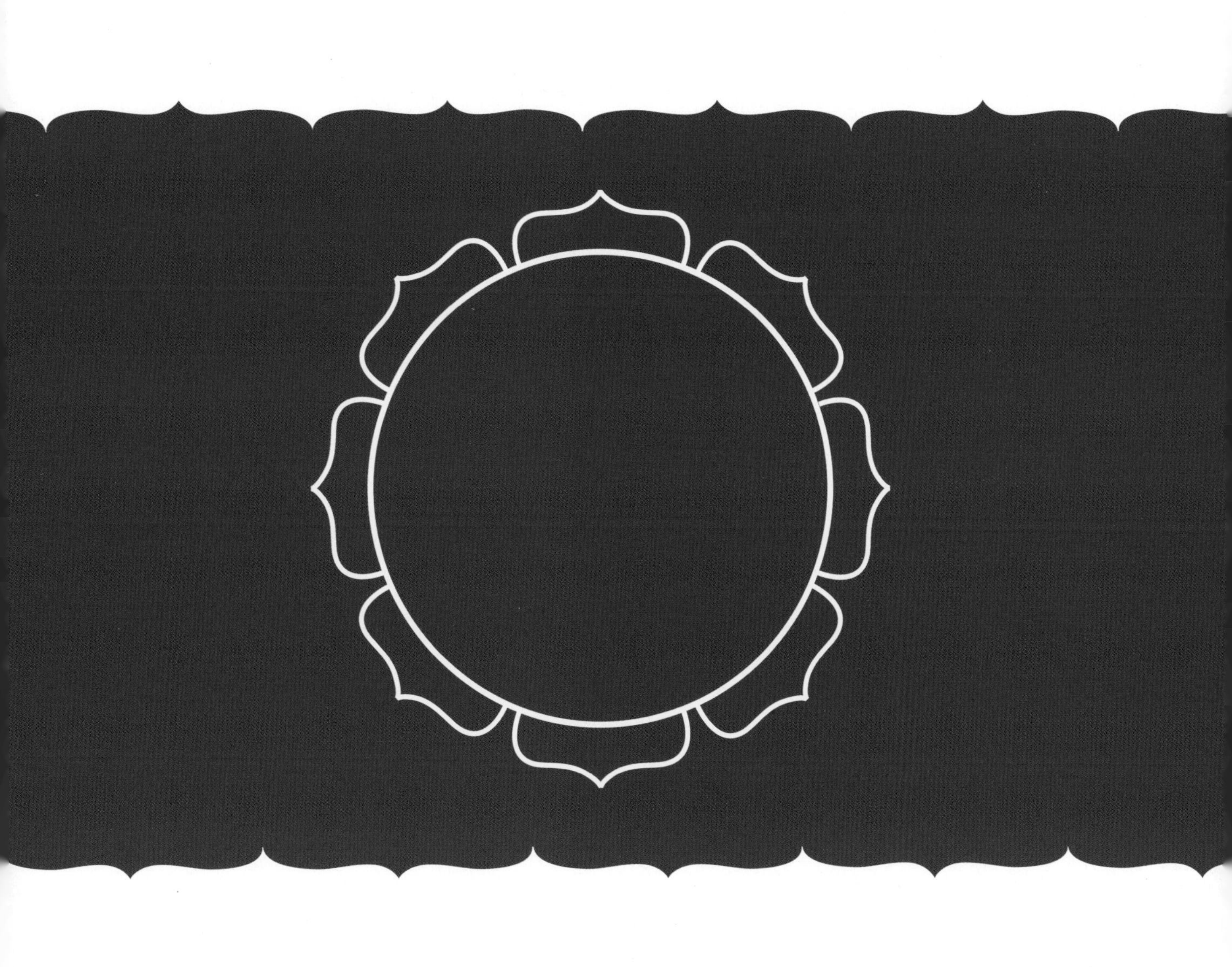

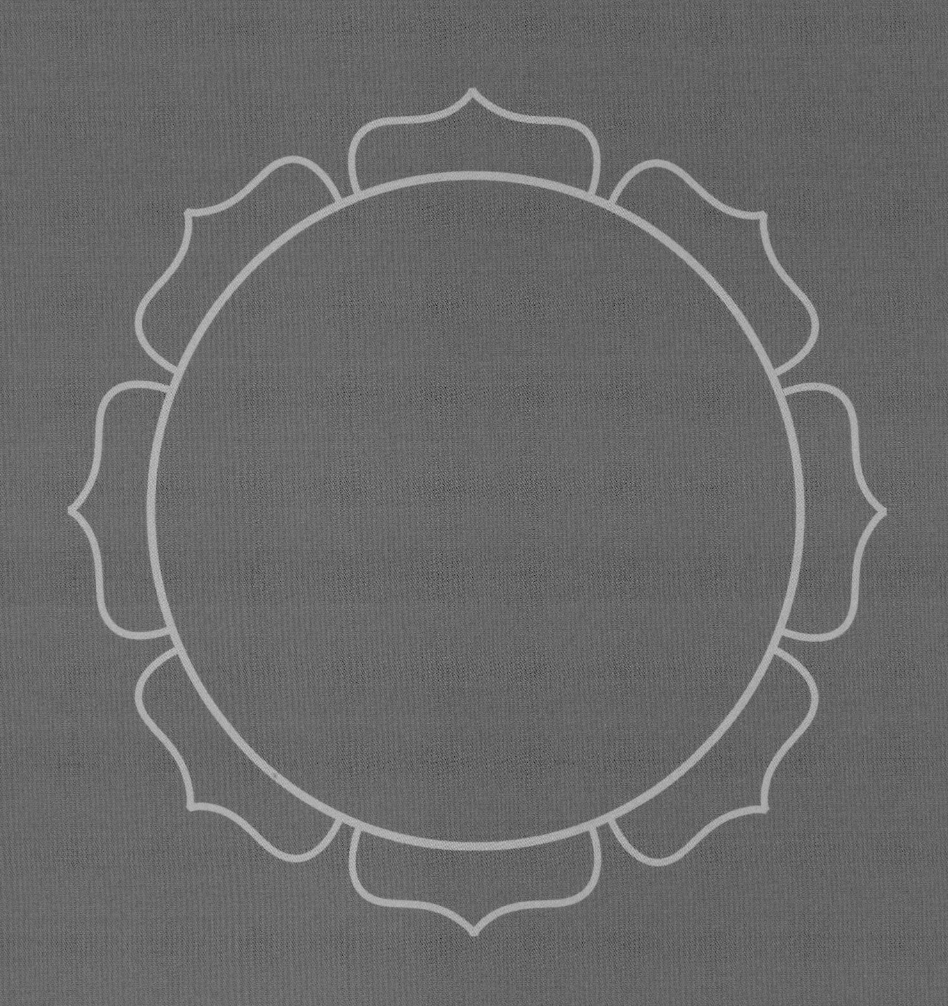

Everything Else

This chapter will give information on many items not covered in all other chapters. These are typical and traditional recipes, unique drinks and dishes, and Indian customs at mealtime. Some recipes will require some ready-made items such as roti, chutney, etc.

Many utensils will be needed for this chapter, as this chapter covers many sorts of dishes. Here are the most useful utensils:

- **Bowls, pots, pans and a nonstick skillet**
- **Spatulas, spoons, and a whisk or hand mixer**
- **Measuring spoons, cups, a cutting board, and knives**

Recipes in This Chapter

Indian Customs at Mealtime

Each region in India may have different customs at mealtime, but the basic philosophy is always the same — hospitality. If you ever go to an Indian home, the custom is that, as a guest, you will be served first. You will also be served more food when you finish, sometimes without asking — and before you know it, you'll have eaten too much. If you want to finish everything on your plate as done in Western countries, it would be advisable to take very little at the beginning. It is not an insult to say, "No thank you," but sometimes the host or hostess will serve you more despite that. It might seem difficult to say "no" without insulting your host. It is okay to ask your host to please let you decide if you want more and promise them that you will do so.

Gol Papdi

This is an Indian sweet that is popular with children and grownups alike. I remember making it every weekend when my children were growing up. Easy to make and tasty, this sweet can be kept in an airtight container for a few days without refrigeration. In the days before refrigeration existed, Indian people would take this sweet when traveling.

The process of making gol papdi takes about 7 to 10 minutes and requires one's full attention, and the mixture will be very hot when it's cooked. This recipe makes about 12 to 16 pieces and serves 4 to 6 people.

Note: Jaggery, also called "gol" or "gur," is minimally processed cane sugar. It is available in Indian markets ground or in powder form, but is best in powder form.

Ingredients:

- 1½ cup whole wheat flour
- ⅔ cup ghee
- ¾ cup jaggery
- 6 almonds, chopped fine

The Process:

Prepare a pie pan or a thali by rubbing about ½ teaspoon of oil inside it so that the gol papdi does not stick. Prepare the jaggery, making sure that it remains in a somewhat powdered form, though small clumps are okay.

Heat the ghee at medium low. Add the flour as soon as the ghee starts to melt. Keep stirring until the flour is covered in ghee and the mixture is soft and loose. Stir often until the flour is cooked and has turned slightly pink. There will be an aroma at that point.

Add the gol and stir until it is melted. The gol should melt right away when added to the hot flour mixture. Turn off the heat and pour the mixture into the pie pan, spreading it evenly with the back of a spoon. Sprinkle almonds on top. Make small squares with a knife while it is still hot and leave until cool.

Take out the gol papdi squares with a pie server. This sweet can be kept in a cool place for a week.

Rolled Roti with Gol

This dish is an all-time favorite for kids and adults alike. My children loved it, and now my granddaughter and her friends love it. It's easy to make and tastes great. It is made of soft roti, butter, and jaggery, which is probably the most minimally processed type of sugar. You can find it in an Indian market.

This treat is very easy to make, especially if you have some leftover roti from a previous meal. You can make fresh roti or buy uncooked roti and jaggery from an Indian market. It is best to buy jaggery in a ground / powdered form. Uncooked roti is available in the refrigerator section of Indian markets.

Make as many of this treat as you want. Typically, a person will eat one or two at a time. This recipe makes 12.

Ingredients:

- 12 roti, cooked or uncooked
- ¼ cup ground jaggery
- 4 teaspoons butter, melted

The Process:

For uncooked roti, heat the skillet and cook each roti for about a minute on each side, until the roti starts puffing and has some spots. Put the roti on a plate. Spread about ½ teaspoon butter on each roti and sprinkle about a teaspoon of gol on top of that. Roll each roti tightly so that the gol does not fall out.

For already-cooked roti, warm one roti on the skillet for a minute, or warm two or three together in the microwave for about 15 seconds.

Note: Recipe can be made vegan by substituting olive oil.

Afterschool Cooler

When your young one comes home on a hot day, try serving this dish and letting him or her pick the fruit to top this sweet Greek yogurt. This is a very healthy snack, and it's colorful, too.

The first time you make this dish, you may want to keep the bowls ready with many choices of fruits. Adding a little syrup on top is also very appealing to children. Use your creativity.

This cool-me-down dish is a great snack for adults as well. Plain Greek yogurt is available in most supermarkets. This dish can be kept ready in the refrigerator. The recipe makes 2 cups and serves up to 4 people.

Ingredients:

- 2 cups plain Greek yogurt
- 2 tablespoons milk
- ½ cup each of diced ripe mangoes, diced peaches, diced strawberries, cut grapes, and pomegranate seedlings
- 2 tablespoons of your child's favorite syrup or agave nectar

The Process:

Whisk the yogurt, milk, and syrup to make a very smooth paste. Put about ½ cup of it into a bowl.

Let the child select two kinds of fruit, then mix the fruit into the yogurt and eat it. Chopped nuts can be added as well.

When your young one comes home on a hot day, try serving this dish and letting him or her pick the fruit to top this sweet Greek yogurt.

Chaash

Chaash is a poor man's probiotic drink that's used by almost all working people in India. It's a great cooling drink for hot days. In India, many farmers go to work with this drink daily. It is quick and easy to make and stays fresh all day.

Salt and roasted jeera or ground black pepper are generally added to chaash. This recipe makes about 4 cups and serves 4 people.

Ingredients:

- 1 cup plain yogurt
- 3 to 4 cups cold water
- ¼ to ½ teaspoon salt
- ¼ teaspoon roasted ground cumin or ground black pepper

The Process:
Put the yogurt in a bowl and add water. Use the hand mixer to make a smooth liquid. Add the salt and roasted cumin powder and serve.

Lassi

This is a modern version of chaash, with varieties of fruits, sugar, and / or syrup added. Lassi is thicker than traditional chaash and is very popular because of its sweetness.

This recipe makes 6 cups and serves 6 to 8 people.

Ingredients:

- 2 cups yogurt (or flavored yogurt, if plain is not available)
- 4 cups water
- ½ cup milk
- 2 to 3 tablespoons sugar
- 1 cup crushed ice

The Process:
Blend all items other than ice together. Pour the mixture into serving glasses. Add ice, top with a piece of fruit, and serve.

Any fruit lassi can be made by blending fruit right into the lassi. For instance...

Mango Lassi:
Use 1 cup chopped mango and 1 tablespoon sugarsugar (or to taste).

Berry Lassi:
Use ½ cup berries and 1 tablespoon sugar (or to taste).

Peach Lassi:
Use 1 cup chopped, skinless peaches and 2 tablespoons sugar.

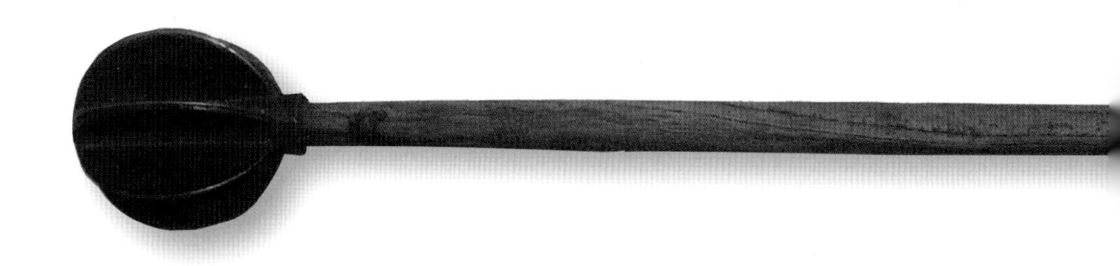

Nimbu Pani / Limbu Pani 

This drink has become very popular in the Indian community. I remember how my mom used to give it to me whenever I had an upset stomach or a fever. She told me that it would help replenish my electrolytes and keep me from getting dehydrated.

Nimbu pani is like a lemonade, but with added salt and black pepper. Additionally, crushed mint will give the drink a beautiful color and taste. This recipe makes about 4 8-ounce glasses and serves 4 to 6 people.

Ingredients:

- 4 cups plain water
- 1 cup sparkling water
- ¼ cup fresh lemon juice
- ½ cup sugar or to taste
- ½ teaspoon salt
- ½ teaspoon crushed black pepper
- 2 tablespoons crushed fresh mint (optional)
- Crushed ice as needed

The Process:

When adding mint, drop ½ teaspoon of mint in gently with a spoon after you pour the limbu pani into a glass. Add a mint sprig.

Roasted Corn on the Cob

This item is sold by street vendors in many countries in Asia. No special utensils are required to make it. Most Western countries rub butter on roasted corn, but this special corn requires a little butter, salt, lemon, chili powder, and chaat masala.

Try serving this dish during a summer party. This dish uses 6 corn cobs without husks.

Ingredients:

- 6 cobs of corn, husked
- Butter
- Lemon juice
- Chili powder
- Chaat masala
- Salt

The Process:

Soak the corn in water before putting it on the grill. Grill the corn by turning it often to avoid burning and popping. Once done, rub it with butter, lemon juice, and then the spices to your liking.

Remove butter to make recipe vegan.

Pudla — Spicy Pancakes 

Breakfast, anyone? This dish is very popular, as it is savory, tasty, and very easy to make. Pudla is like an omelet without eggs, and it is gluten-free. It makes a great change from regular pancakes. Serve it with your favorite chutney. Many people serve it with tomato ketchup.

This recipe serves 4 to 6 people and makes about 12 small pancakes. Serve the pancakes as you make them fresh.

Ingredients:

- 2 cups chickpea flour or besan
- 3 cups water
- 2 tablespoons lemon juice
- 1 teaspoon salt
- 1 cup each of chopped onions, tomatoes, and cilantro
- ½ teaspoon baking soda
- 1 teaspoon ajwain seeds (or anise seeds)
- 4 tablespoons oil
- 1 teaspoon salt
- ¼ teaspoon turmeric
- ½ finely chopped green chili

The Process:

Mix the besan and water with a whisk or a hand mixer so that there are no lumps. Add all of the spices and chopped items. Add the soda and lemon juice and whisk again. Add about a tablespoon of oil and mix.

Heat the flat skillet. Add about a teaspoon of oil when the skillet is hot – about 1 to 2 minutes on medium high heat. Pour about a quarter cup of ready batter onto the hot skillet. It will spread like a pancake and bubble. Turn it over when cooked and serve hot with your favorite chutney or sweet chili sauce. You can make large or small pudla depending on what you like.

Upma

This is South Indian savory dish made with semolina (cream of wheat). This dish can be served at any time and can be made ahead of time and warmed before serving. It is very easy and quick to make. Serve it with coconut chutney or green chutney if you like it spicy. Upma rava (roasted large sooji) semolina is available at Indian markets. If this variety is not available, you can use regular sooji. This recipe makes about 2 to 3 cups and serves 4 to 6 people.

Ingredients:

- 1½ cup sooji (semolina)
- 2 cups of water
- 1 cup plain yogurt (lowfat is okay)
- 3 tablespoons oil
- ½ onion, chopped
- 1 chopped green chili (or to taste)
- 1 teaspoon urad daal
- 4 curry leaves
- 1 teaspoon panch puran
- ¼ cup chopped cilantro
- 2 teaspoons green chutney (optional)

The Process:

Heat a deep nonstick pan. Add the sooji and stir often to make sure that it is properly roasted. The sooji will turn slightly darker when roasted. Pour it into a bowl. Mix the water and yogurt in another bowl, whisking to remove any lumps.

In the same pan, heat oil for about a minute. Add the urad daal. When it starts to change color, add panch puran, letting it crackle or fry for about a minute. Add the curry leaves, onions, and chili. Cook for about 2 to 3 minutes.

Add the roasted sooji and mix well, then add the yogurt mixture. Caution: The yogurt may splatter when it is added to the hot mixture. Add the salt and let the mixture cook, stirring occasionally. It can be covered partially while cooking, but keep the heat low. When almost all of the liquid has evaporated, close the lid and continue cooking it for about 3 to 5 minutes.

Add cilantro and mix before serving. Serve hot. This dish can be reheated. Serving suggestion: Top it with green or coconut chutney.

Sago and Potato Khicheri

This is a very popular dish that is mainly made during certain festivals. Many people just eat this item on certain fasting days when no grain is used. You can eat this dish as a snack or mix it with yogurt to make a meal.

Potatoes, sago, and peanuts are this dish's main ingredients. Two sizes of sago are available in Indian markets. I use the larger size.

Note: Soak the sago before you boil the potatoes. The potatoes should be slightly firm. Their boiling time depends on the kind of potatoes that you use. It takes about 10 minutes for red potatoes. Use almonds if you are allergic to peanuts.

This dish can be kept in the refrigerator for about 3 to 4 days and can be reheated. The recipe makes about 4 to 5 cups and serves 4 to 6 people.

Ingredients:

- 6 medium potatoes, boiled and cut into ¼- to ½-inch cubes with their skin removed
- 3 cups water to soak sago
- 1½ cups sago, soaked in 3 cups of water before boiling potatoes
- 3 tablespoons oil
- 2 tablespoons lemon juice
- 1 tablespoon sugar
- 2 tablespoons roasted ground cumin
- 1 green chili with the seeds removed and chopped very finely (for a spicier taste)
- 1 teaspoon ground black pepper
- 6 curry leaves
- 1 cup roasted and chopped peanuts
- ¼ cup chopped cilantro

The Process:

Boil the potatoes. After they're boiled, remove their skins and cut them into small cubes.

After soaking, the sago will have doubled in quantity. Wash it and drain the excess water with a strainer.

Heat oil in a large nonstick pan or a wok-like skillet. Add the chopped chili and curry leaves. Add the cubed potatoes and stir gently.

Add the soaked sago, salt, sugar, and lemon juice. Stir gently until well-mixed. Add the roasted cumin powder and black pepper.

Add the peanuts and cilantro and mix before serving.

Pav Bhaji

"Pav" means "bread" and "bhaji" means "vegetables." This dish can be a meal or a snack, but it is typically made as a meal. There are two kinds of pav bhaji: one in which the base ingredient is mashed potatoes, and one that uses many vegetables. A special spice mixture gives this dish a unique spicy taste. You can use your choice of bread with this dish, heating it with butter on a skillet.

The special masala for this recipe, pav bhaji masala, can be purchased at an Indian market. The masala comes in small packets, which will be more than you will need. Your other option is to use the masala in the recipe. This recipe serves 4 to 6 people. The ingredients below are for the potato variety of pav bhaji.

Ingredients:

- 4 potatoes, boiled and partially mashed
- 2 tomatoes, chopped
- 1 tablespoon tomato paste
- 1 large onion, finely chopped
- 2 tablespoons chopped cilantro (for garnish)
- 1 teaspoon salt
- 1 tablespoon lemon juice
- 2 tablespoons oil
- ½ teaspoon each of black mustard and cumin seeds
- 2 tablespoons coriander-cumin powder
- 1 clove garlic or ½ teaspoon minced garlic
- 1 teaspoon amchoor
- ½ teaspoon each of garam masala and chili powder

The Process:

In a skillet or a wok-like pan, heat oil for about a minute, then add the seeds, onion, garlic, and tomatoes. Cook until the mixture is very soft. Add the tomato paste and mix well. Add the semi-mashed potatoes and then all of the spices. Taste the mixture to check if it needs more spices.

Let it simmer for about 10 minutes. In the meantime, heat a flat skillet, butter the slices of breads, and roast them on each side.

Turn off the heat on the potato mixture. Add the lemon juice, then stir and garnish with cilantro. Serve with the butter-roasted bread.

Note: Recipe can be made vegan by substituting olive oil.

Khada Pav Bhaji or Kadai Pav Bhaji

Khada pav bhaji (Kadai pav bhaji) really means that the bhaji is cooked on an open flat skillet. This dish uses a lot of vegetables rather than just potatoes as a base. Because of the variety of vegetables used, this has a very special and rich flavor.

Ingredients:

- 1 potato, peeled and chopped
- 3-inch cauliflower floret, chopped
- 1 small zucchini, chopped
- 4-inch Chinese eggplant, chopped
- ¼ cup green peas and carrots mix (frozen is okay)
- ¼ cup finely chopped green beans

The Process:

All other items in the ingredients are the same.

As with pav bhaji, heat the oil and then add the tomatoes, onions, garlic, and tomato paste.

Add the vegetables and stir fry them until soft. You may need to add about 2 tablespoons of water if the mixture is too dry and sticks to the bottom of the pan.

Roast the bread with butter on each side. Garnish the vegetable bhaji and serve it.

Note: Recipe can be made vegan by substituting olive oil.

Yogurt

Yogurt is generally made in most households daily. It is consumed on daily basis.

The process is very simple. You do not need any yogurt maker. Yogurt takes about 8 hours to form.

I do this process at night and by morning the yogurt is ready.

Yogurt is made with culture and to make it, you must have fresh culture – just like some breads.

It is important to buy small container of fresh plain yogurt without additives.

I use a steel pot to boil and make yogurt in the same pot-pan.

Utensils:

- A pan to boil milk
- A cover for the pot and a towel to wrap around the pan
- A whisk

Ingredients:

- 2 cups plain milk – lowfat or regular
- 3 tablespoons of ready purchase plain yogurt, whisked

The Process:

Heat milk in the pan at low medium heat, bring it to one boil, and turn off the heat.

Remove the pan and let the milk cool to warm. It must be warm to the touch, not hot.

Add the whisked yogurt and mix it into the milk with a whisk. I mix gently with my fingers to make sure that the yogurt is thoroughly mixed with the milk.

Now put the pot in a warm place. I keep it in the oven on a rack. Cover the pot with a lid and wrap it with a towel. Keep it undisturbed for about 8 hours. Just make sure not to turn on the oven.

The yogurt will be formed.

Keep fresh yogurt in the refrigerator and use as needed for many dishes.

Making Yogurt

Making Greek Yogurt

Note: To make Greek yogurt, put a cup of plain yogurt in a muslin cloth and let the water drain for about 2 hours (see photo). A cup of plain yogurt makes about ½ cup of Greek yogurt. Mix it with your favorite fruit, add a little Agave nectar and you have a wonderful snack.

Ghee

Ghee is easy to make at home, but it is important to heat it at the right temperature and time. One pound of butter takes about 15 minutes at low-simmer heat.

Utensils:

- 1 heavy pan-stainless steel would be great.
- Pot holders
- 1 strainer
- 1 Mason or other jar to hold about 2 cups of liquid

Ingredients:

- 1 pound unsalted butter.

The Process:

Slice all 4 sticks of butter in ½-inch pats. Put them in the pan (preferably stainless steel) and turn on heat at low-simmer. As butter melts, it may splatter a little, so keep watchful eyes. When all the butter is melted, it will form foam on top – do not scoop it out. It will then bubble. Let it simmer until the bubbles are gone, take the pan off the heat, and turn off the heat source.

Timing is important. Make sure the ghee color is yellow. When it is cool, strain it in to a jar and cover it when it has completely cooled.

Ghee can be kept in the pantry for about 2 to 3 months.

Basic Curry Sauce

Indian food is associated with curry and spice, and many regions make varieties of curry.

This recipe is a basic sauce which can be made ahead of time and kept in small containers in the freezer. Use them as needed. This recipe makes about 3 to 4 cups of curry sauce.

Ingredients:

- 4 to 6 medium onions, finely chopped
- 2 to 3 cups of water
- 4 large tomatoes, chopped
- 2 tablespoons of tomato paste
- 1 and a half teaspoon garlic paste
- 3 Tablespoons coriander-cumin powder
- 2½ teaspoons ginger-chili paste
- 3 tablespoons raw cashews
- 3 tablespoons oil

The Process:

In a pan large enough to hold about 6 cups, heat oil for about 1 minute over medium heat.

Add onions and lower the heat, cook the onions till they are translucent and slightly brown — about 5 minutes.

Add tomatoes and cook for another 4 to 5 minutes. Now add the rest of the items. Let the mixture cook for about 20 to 30 minutes at medium heat.

Once the mixture cools, blend it well and make a paste. This recipe makes about 3 to 4 cups.

Pour this sauce in containers to store when cool.

Acknowledgments

My inspiration came from my husband, my children, and my grandchildren who still enjoy my roti fresh from the griddle.

This book is created for the next generation. I have cooked each and every recipe in my own kitchen.

I really would like to thank everyone who has helped create this book — my husband and my children and their spouses. Special thanks to Steve Bass who designed this book first. Many thanks to friends of my children who have eaten food I cooked for years. Thanks to my sisters, our family, our friends, and everyone who has encouraged me to create new recipes. This is a family cookbook, and my children and grandchildren have helped me at every stage.

This has been a dream and a long hard road.

To my teacher and designer, Jerry – I could not have done it without you.

Index

P

R